The Official
Los Angeles Lakers
Yearbook '90 - '91

by Roland Lazenby

photographs by NBA Photos

TAYLOR PUBLISHING COMPANY
Dallas, Texas

Design by Karen Snidow Lazenby

©1990, Roland Lazenby
Taylor Publishing Company
1550 West Mockingbird Lane, Dallas, Texas 75235

ISBN 0-87833-764-4

Printed in the United States of America

(Andrew Bernstein photos)

Contents

Preface

Welcome to the first edition of the Los Angeles Lakers yearbook. It reflects the efforts and involvement of many people.

First in line is Bob Steiner, director of public relations for California Sports, Inc. (the parent company that owns the Lakers). Many thanks also go to the Lakers' public relations staff—John Black and Stacy Brown, who compiled the information for Laker Profiles and wrote the bios, and to their assistants, Matt Fleer and Lani Hana.

A number of people were gracious in granting interviews, including Jerry West, Magic Johnson, James Worthy, Mike Dunleavy, Jamaal Wilkes, Pat Riley, Elgin Baylor, Bob Cousy, Red Auerbach, Chris Ford, Larry Bird, Gerald Henderson, Kevin McHale, Robert Parish, K.C. Jones, Isiah Thomas, and Chuck Daly.

Of tremendous value was *Winnin' Times,* the excellent book on the Lakers by Steve Springer and Scott Ostler. Other books used as reference include: *50 Years of the Final Four* by Billy Packer and Roland Lazenby; *100 Greatest Basketball Players* by Wayne Patterson and Lisa Fisher; *Championship NBA* by Leonard Koppett; *College Basketball's 25 Greatest Teams* by Billy Packer and Roland Lazenby; *Giant Steps* by Kareem Abdul-Jabbar and Peter Knobler; *Magic's Touch* by Magic Johnson and Roy S. Johnson; *March to the Top* by Art Chansky and Eddie Fogler; *Rick Barry's Pro Basketball Scouting Report* by Rick Barry and Jordan E. Cohn; *Showtime,* by Pat Riley and Byron Laursen; *The Bird Era* by Bob Schron and Kevin Stevens; *The Official NBA Basketball Encyclopedia*, edited by Zander Hollander and Alex Sachare; *The Story of Basketball* by Dave Anderson; and *The NBA Finals* by Roland Lazenby.

This project would be drab were it not for the photographic contributions of Andrew Bernstein, Nathaniel Butler, Jon Soohoo, Al Gonzalez, Barry Gossage, Steve Grayson, Steve Lipofsky, Ron Koch, and Kirthmon Dozier. Also vital was the effort of Kristan Kanost of NBA Photos.

Extensive use was made of a variety of publications, including *The Orange County Register, USA Today, The New York Times, The Detroit News, The Detroit Free Press, Los Angeles Times, Los Angeles Herald Examiner, The Boston Globe, Boston Herald, The National, Sports Illustrated,* and *The Sporting News.*

I also made great use of the fine reporting efforts of the following writers: Dave Anderson, Frank DeFord, David Dupree, Scott Ostler, Bob Ryan, Roy S. Johnson, Ted Green, Dave Kindred, Mitch Chortkoff, Pat Putnam, Sandy Padwe, Jack McCallum, Sam McManis, Doug Cress, Mike Littwin, John Papanek, Leonard Lewin, Leonard Koppett, George Vecsey, Alex Wolff, Bruce Newman, Steve Bulpett, and Allen Greenberg.

In addition, Pat Steele of D.M. Steele Company in Fullerton, California, provided the typesetting for the records pages.

I also owe much to the book's primary editor, Jim Donovan at Taylor Publishing, and the staff at Taylor.

Roland Lazenby
October 1990

A.C. in action. (Nathaniel Butler photo)

Dunleavy was a much-valued assistant in Milwaukee.

Going For The Glue

As youth movements go, this may not have been exactly what the fans had in mind. But youth is exactly what the Los Angeles Lakers and Boston Celtics accomplished last June when they hired rookie head coaches.

The teams' new bosses—Mike Dunleavy in Los Angeles and Chris Ford in Boston—have little or no bench experience whatsoever. Both have spent considerable time as assistant coaches, but, as Ford points out, "things change when you move over that 12 inches on the bench to the head spot."

At face value, it seems almost preposterous. How could the National Basketball Association's most storied franchises put their fortunes in the hands of untested coaches? But face value has never mattered much with the Celtics and Lakers. Time after time, these two teams have shown a flair for taking the unorthodox and making it work. Which means there probably won't be any lines forming for people placing bets against them this time, either.

After all, it's been done before. As Lakers General Manager Jerry West points out, both Paul Westhead and Pat Riley won championships in Los Angeles as rookie head coaches.

As the cynical line goes, it's a players' game, so coaches aren't all that important anyway. After all, aren't Larry Bird and Magic Johnson the real coaches of their teams?

The reality, though, is a bit more complicated than that. Coaching does matter in the NBA, it just doesn't matter as much as it does in college. And it matters more than it ever has, because defense is more of a factor in the league today.

Coaching in the NBA, in fact, is a very fine art. There is no better

Both Paul Westhead and Pat Riley won championships in Los Angeles as rookie head coaches.

example than that of the two previous coaches of the Lakers and Celtics.

Pat Riley had practiced that fine art for nine seasons in Los Angeles, long enough to coach the Lakers to seven appearances in the NBA Finals and four championships, a record that left him with more playoff wins (102) than any coach in league history. Then last season, he prodded the team along to a league-best 63 wins during the regular season and capped off the campaign by winning his first NBA Coach of the Year award. But the Lakers faltered against Phoenix in the playoffs, and in the aftermath Riley decided to move on to NBC as a broadcaster.

After all, nine seasons is an eternity in the modern NBA.

In Boston, coach Jimmy Rodgers went out with a winning record, but he

went out just the same. When Boston lost to the New York Knicks in the first round of the playoffs, Celtics President Red Auerbach and team management decided to replace Rodgers after his second season on the job.

Now, in starting over with young coaches, each team is looking for something different, but they both want the same results—just the right coaching touch to coax another championship out of their rosters.

"We're not interested in being competitive," Auerbach says of Ford's first Celtic team. "We're interested in winning it."

The Lakers, of course, are taking the same approach. "Results are what we're interested in," West declared in a recent interview.

Actually, it should come as no shock that these two teams have begun their 1990s rebuilding process with a similar approach. For three decades now, the Lakers and Celtics have moved through the NBA in a lockstep, their dynasties rising and falling with an almost eerie cadence. Their first clashes came during the 1960s when the young Lakers, featuring West and Elgin Baylor, battled the Bill Russell-led Celtics. Then, in 1979, Magic and Larry began moving their teams to a furious beat. Boston won three world championships in the 1980s, and Los Angeles won five.

But, as cozy as their twosome was, the Celtics and Lakers have been interrupted over the last few seasons. Neither team has won a championship in two years while the Detroit Pistons have ruled the league. It's been a long time since either team has had a losing record, but merely winning isn't enough in Boston or Los Angeles.

> **"We'd rather take our chances on somebody young and bright and enthusiastic and innovative, somebody you can work with."**
>
> **—Jerry West**

"In Boston, we have the sophisticated fans," Ford said. "Their only concern is if you hang a banner up at the end of the year."

Although he's eager to take the job, he's also very much aware that there is only so much an NBA coach can do. "There were a lot of things that arose that Jimmy had no control over," he said in Rodgers' defense.

Dealing with players in today's big-money environment will be his major challenge, Ford said. "A big key will be to get them to see what the team good is, particularly now with the lucrative contracts making it even tougher to get them to focus."

That would seem to be a pungent issue in Los Angeles because the Lakers lured unrestricted free agent forward Sam Perkins away from Dallas in August. Perkins' new six-year contract is said to run in excess of $18 million, but West hasn't even blinked at those numbers.

"They simply have to go that way when the league guarantees its players 53 percent of its revenue," he said.

Any inequities in the league's pay scale will work themselves out, West said. "We have an owner here [Dr. Jerry Buss in Los Angeles] who obviously takes care of his players."

West understandably bristles at questions about his selection of a coach. Why recycle another older coach? he asked. "We'd rather take our chances on somebody young and bright and enthusiastic and innovative, somebody you can work with."

From all accounts, the 36-year-old Dunleavy is certainly that. He has

Boston's new coach, Chris Ford, with son Michael. (Steve Lipofsky photo)

played for and served under Milwaukee coach Del Harris and Golden State's Don Nelson. That experience and his low-key but effective personal style have made him a hot property around the league. He had turned down at least two other head coaching jobs and numerous assistants offers before agreeing to join the Lakers in June.

Still, his selection was something of a surpise in Los Angeles, so Dunleavy doesn't take the questions about his lack of experience as an affront. "I take it as a compliment," he said. "They could have chosen probably anybody in the league. Anybody would have loved to have this job. So would a lot of top college coaches. Any time there's a team with a lot of success and tradition, people want to be associated with it."

Actually both Ford and Dunleavy fit a long-established mold for coaching success. They were both "glue men" as players, valuable to their teams not as superstars but as solid, consistent performers, able to play defense and contribute just enough on offense. Glue men typically average five to 10 years in the league and score an average of seven to 12 points per game over their careers. Ford, who has the distinction of making the first three-pointer in NBA history, averaged 9.2 points a game over 10 years. For Dunleavy, who became something of a three-point specialist while playing for Philadelphia, Houston, San Antonio and Milwaukee, the numbers were 8.0 points over 10 years.

A look at the honor roll of coaches who have taken teams to the Finals

Perkins is the new addition. (Dallas Mavericks photo)

Dunleavy goes to the hole for Philly in the 1977 Finals. (Ron Koch photo)

means they see a variety of coaching styles. "I played for eight different coaches in 10 years," Ford said. The list runs from K.C. Jones to Dick Vitale, and Ford said he has learned from all of them.

The main lesson?

"You need a great working relationship with the players," he said.

Dunleavy agreed and stressed that the relationship needed to be with all the players, not just the superstars.

West cautions that a coach can't bear too much of the responsibility. It's a players game, and ultimately the players will determine the team's success, he said. "A coach is an important factor in a championship team, but not the most important factor. You have to have the players."

In that sense, the pressure is on the Lakers' front office, not Dunleavy, to get the players, West said. "If we can bring him the right people, then he should have a good chance for success."

To that end, West made a series of dazzling roster moves during the offseason. Unsure that he would make the team, veteran guard Michael Cooper moved on to play in Italy, and West dealt backup forward Orlando Woolridge to Denver.

Those moves created room enough in the salary cap to allow him to sign Perkins and pick up guard Terry Teagle from Golden State. Most observers seem to agree the acquisitions should make the Lakers better, although you wonder how much improvement you can make on a 63-win season.

"This should be a terrific team," West said. "Maybe even better than

shows that the majority of them have a similar profile. Al Attles (8.9 points over 11 seasons), K.C. Jones (7.4 over nine seasons), Alex Hannum (6.0 over nine), Larry Costello (12.2 over 12), Pat Riley (7.4 over nine), Red Holzman (9.4 over nine), George Senesky (7.2 over eight), Paul Seymour (9.4 over 15), Fred Schaus (12.2 over five), Gene Shue (14.4 over 10), Rick Adelman (7.7 over seven) and Al Cervi (9.4 over 9) were all relatively average players who went on to accomplish great things as coaches. Between them, the teams they coached have made 31 trips to the Finals and come away with 14 championships.

The reasons that glue men make good coaches are fairly obvious, Dunleavy said. "More than likely, they've had to survive and succeed

on more than athletic ability."

"We were probably sound fundamentally although we weren't superstars," Ford agreed.

They were the kinds of players who had to know their team's system in and out, Dunleavy said, and they had to play defense. Because they weren't always as quick, they had to know the opponent's systems and tendencies. "I had to know where my guy was going before he made his move," Dunleavy said.

As a result of the extra work they put in, the glue men got a complete look at the game, which meant they had the basic knowledge to become coaches. They had learned to formulate their ideas and copy from others.

Also, average players tend to move around in their careers, which

Dunleavy and wife Emily with Dr. Jerry Buss, owner of the Lakers. (Jon Soohoo photo)

last year."

The circumstances mean that Dunleavy's challenge will be rapid assembly. He'll have to get them all playing together quickly. Going into the season, he plans to start second-year Yugoslavian center Vlade Divac with A.C. Green and James Worthy in the frontcourt, while bringing the $18-million Perkins off the bench.

"It's a matter of how quickly we can bring it all together," Dunleavy said.

Two weaknesses emerged last season with the Lakers. They struggled to score with their half-court offense, and on defense they were vulnerable to smaller, quicker guards. People in Los Angeles have been reluctant to say it, but Dunleavy isn't. The Lakers missed Kareem Abdul-Jabbar, who retired after the 1989 season, he said. "I think there was a void there. Basically with Kareem in your lineup, you could always get a shot."

The 6'9" Perkins won't solve that

Dunleavy challenged Walton in the '77 Finals. (Koch Photo)

Even as he speaks positively, Dunleavy knows that he and Ford, two former long-range gunners, are now faced with a short-range hustle.

problem by himself, but the Lakers see him as a marvelously versatile player, capable of playing power forward, center or small forward.

The 30-year-old Teagle is equally versatile, having played both big guard and small forward for the Warriors. He's big and strong (6'5", 190 pounds) and can leap. With his offensive skills, he likes to post up and score. His defensive intensity has improved in recent seasons, and he has adapted well to being a bench player. He doesn't complain. He's not a great ballhandler, but should see playing time when the Lakers need some offensive punch.

The other newcomers are first-round pick Elden Campbell out of Clemson and guard Tony Smith from Marquette. The Lakers first questioned the 6'11" Campbell's intensity last season when they scouted him in college. But he's made a good early showing in Los Angeles. "He's been terrific so far," Dunleavy said. "He's been very coachable, and he's got more skills than I thought he had. He's very capable of blocking shots, he's got terrific hands and runs the floor well."

The 6'4" Smith has impressed the Lakers, too. "I think he'll be an NBA player for a long time," West said.

But Dunleavy wants a low-pressure introduction for both rookies. If they can help the team right away, that's fine, he said. But if they can't, the Lakers will more than likely be patient. With Mychal Thompson 35, Magic 31 and Worthy 29, the team has an eye on the future.

Besides, Dunleavy has a strong sense that the veterans are primed to deliver. The new coach said that

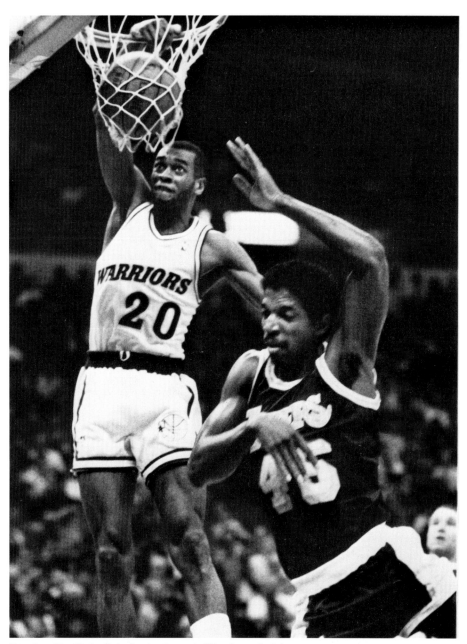
Teagle will add depth to the backcourt. (Warriors photo)

shortly after taking the job he had "terrific meetings" with Magic, Worthy, Byron Scott and Larry Drew. They all seemed very eager for the upcoming season, he said. "And I don't think they were just saying the right thing. I think they really believed it. I think that rebounding from last year's loss in the playoffs is a matter of personal pride for all of them. I think they were all disappointed."

Even as he speaks positively, Dunleavy knows that he and Ford, two former long-range gunners, are now faced with a short-range hustle. That doesn't seem to bother either one of them.

Ford recalled that as a starter for Boston he faced Dunleavy, then playing for Houston, in the 1981 Finals. "We both had nice careers, and we played against each other in the Finals," Ford said. "Fortunately my team won. Hopefully we'll get to meet there again."

"I'd go for that," Dunleavy said in a blink.

Spoken, perhaps, with the youthful enthusiasm of rookies, but—heading into the '90s—that may be just what these two teams need.

Dunleavy plans to start Divac. (Barry Gossage photo)

Worthy works on Bird in the 1987 Finals. (Bernstein photos)

Just James

Posted up.

The shot blocker.

Y ou're the defender, and you can't help but notice James Worthy's left leg. He's got all his weight on it, and it's quivering like a bowstring. He keeps pressing harder on it, working the ball of his foot against the wood, searching for that special spot that will give him the maximum lift.

Here you are, 16 feet from the basket, just left of the key, and he's got you posted up. Posted up and searching for lift! Way the hell out here on the perimeter. Just you and him.

Which way is he going!?!

He's got his back to you, the ball sits snugly in his right palm, extended out from his body, just out of your reach. He's peering back over his left shoulder, looking right through you to the hoop. All the while he keeps flicking the ball to his right. He's twitching it actually. Teasing you with the ball. Twitch right. Twitch right. Look left.

Which way will he go?

What you really want to do is back up just a little more, to stop his drive. But you can't give him the open 16-footer.

Whatever you do, don't panic. Don't freeze up.

Remember. The left leg is the key. The quivering increases like a rocket before liftoff. He's going to push off it and explode right to the baseline and jam it in your face. Embarrassment time. You know it. The only question is when. How long can he wait? It seems like an eternity. You allow yourself one quick glance at the shotclock. 10. 9.

Suddenly his head jerks hard right, and that's it. You go for it.

Just as quickly, he shifts his weight to his right foot and explodes back to the left. Now how the hell can he do that? There he goes, and here you are.

He moves swiftly into the lane. It's wide open. The help-side defense is as surprised as you are. The help arrives, but it's too late. He flips up a little eight-foot shot. Good. And to make matters worse, the late help fouls him. Three-point play.

And where are you? Out in the flats somewhere looking for your lingerie.

At 6'9" Worthy makes a big target. (Bernstein photo)

The quickness makes him deadly.

Not afraid to scrap.

Celebrating the '85 title with wife Angela. (Bernstein photos)

The moves and fakes always seem to come with a new variation, but James Worthy's quickness has been creating that same kind of motion sickness in his opponents for a few years now.

Perhaps it would be easier for them if after each little sequence, he would smile, show just a trace of gloating. Something to fire them up.

But it's always the same blank assassin's stare. Nothing personal, bub. Just doin' the job.

"He's got that great gift," says Lakers General Manager Jerry West, "that ability to shoot the ball very quickly. And he's got an incredible first step. He's got an advantage over most people he plays against with that quickness and the ability to shoot the ball with both hands. He's one of the players you can't really defend. You just hope to contain him."

Worthy's game is so subtle, it's difficult for the fan to pick up the little intricacies of his play, West said.

The accompanying photographs may help a bit. They show just how special Worthy's game is.

The acrobat. (Soohoo photo)

The quick shot. (Gossage photo)

Worthy at Carolina. (UNC photo)

Worthy was the Most Outstanding Player in the 1982 Final Four. (Georgetown University photo)

He can shoot right or left. (Bernstein photos)

The team player.

Face job.

Showtimers.

It's over.

The Showtime teams are the greatest ever. (Steve Grayson photo)

The Greatest Show On Earth?

Who is the greatest basketball player of all time? That's an impossible question. About the best you can hope to do is list the top half dozen candidates. Researchers at the Naismith Memorial Basketball Hall of Fame did just that in 1989. They picked the top 100 players in the history of the game. For their top six, they chose:

1 Wilt Chamberlain
2. Kareem Abdul-Jabbar
3. Bill Russell
4. Larry Bird
5. Oscar Robertson
6. Earvin Johnson

Such a list is sure to stir debate among Laker fans. But whether or not you agree with the ranking, it does offer one reassuring fact: Two of the members—Earvin and Kareem—played on the same team. That, of course, would be Showtime, the 1979-89 Lakers. And the seventh player on the list, Jerry West, served as the club's general manager for much of that decade.

Plus there was more. Laker forward James Worthy was ranked number 34 on the list. And Jamaal Wilkes, another Laker forward for part of the decade, pulled in at number 60.

It's no wonder that the Lakers made it to the NBA Finals eight times in those 10 years and won five championships.

As angry as you may be with the individual selections, you have to admit that the list is another piece of evidence suggesting that the Showtime Lakers were the greatest basketball team ever.

If the Magic/Kareem edition of the Lakers isn't the greatest team of all time, it is at least the greatest team in pro basketball's modern era. No group of men has ever played the game better.

You'd probably get quite a heated protest if you launched such a notion within earshot of a certain cigar-puffing, former redhead. Arnold Auerbach thinks his Bill Russell-led Celtics of 1957-69 vintage were the greatest team ever. They won 11 championships in 13 years, didn't they?

Russell's Celtics and Kareem Abdul-Jabbar's Lakers never came face to face on a basketball court, but Auerbach has spent a little time sitting around his Washington, D.C. office imagining what their meeting would have wrought. A writer pointed out that at least one basketball computer program has suggested that Kareem's team might have won.

As would be expected, Auerbach rejected such a notion with a puff of smoke. "Computers," he said, "can never creep into peoples' competitive attitudes. Not that Abdul-Jabbar wasn't a great competitor. But Russell continually rose to occasions. Abdul-Jabbar did, too. Abdul-Jabbar was a giant among men, he was so much

bigger than everybody else. What would have happened if they were playing face to face? I don't know. Russell would have devised something to affect that sky hook. Look at how Russell adjusted against Chamberlain. To me he outplayed Chamberlain nine out of 10 times."

Bob Cousy, who played point guard for six of Auerbach's championship teams, agrees with his former coach about Russell. "Kareem was more talented," Cousy said. "But when the whistle blew, Russell became an animal."

Cousy, though, has a different opinion about the team matchup. If the '61 Celtics played the '87 Lakers, the guys in the purple and gold shorts would probably take it, he said. "Out of seven games, we'd certainly win two of them. We might even steal a third."

Still, Cousy admitted that given a few beers, he might change his opinion.

Whatever the perspective, such debates will smoulder until somebody invents a time machine that allows teams from one era to lace up their sneakers against teams from another era.

In the meantime we have to deal with the certainties, and this much is a certainty.

If the Magic/Kareem edition of the Lakers isn't the greatest team of all time, it is at least the greatest team in pro basketball's modern era. No group of men has ever played the game better.

Jerry West has one of the best

Kareem led the Bucks to the Finals twice. (Koch photo)

sensed was a battle of emerging superstars, one black, the other white. In a sense, they both confirmed and shattered stereotypes every time they played. Larry Bird was white and raised in near poverty in a family torn apart by alcohol abuse. Earvin Johnson was black, the product of a stable middle-class home where both parents worked to provide their children with the advantages.

As a player, Johnson was considered a fleet, infinitely talented blue-chipper. In reality, he wasn't much of a jumper and had virtually no outside shot, yet he had honed his skills with endless hours on the playgrounds. The product of his effort was a truly unique big man, fluid enough to play point guard brilliantly.

Bird was considered slow and lead-footed, unable to jump. He even played that angle up a bit at the 1979 Final Four. "I've never considered myself a super athlete," he told reporters. "I admit I'm not the quickest guy in the world. In fact, I'm slow. But I've always tried to make up for that in other ways. I block out and I follow up shots for rebounds. And if there's a loose ball on the floor, I'll be down there bumping heads."

It sounded nice, but in reality, Bird was a marvelously gifted athlete who worked constantly to improve his natural ability.

To that end, both players used any and every possible edge they could find. Rather than be hindered by the stereotypes they faced, both had the smarts to turn them into powerful weapons and motivational tools.

"We're both the same," Johnson would later admit. "We'll do anything to win. You can list all the great players you want, but there are only a couple of winners."

Almost from the start of their relationship, Larry and Earvin were cast as basketball's Odd Couple. Eventually, the writers would come to describe them as "inextricably linked," but the two really didn't care much for each other in the early days of their rivalry. Magic was an easygoing kid with dancing eyes and a quick smile. He naturally liked people and was

basketball minds ever, and the thought of Magic and Kareem on the same team still blows him away.

"That's incredible," he said.

THE STRANGEST OF PAIRINGS

Perhaps the best thing about the Lakers' dominance is that it came during pro basketball's Camelot days. The 1980s had a legendary, magical aura about them that projected the NBA into the imagination of mainstream America. Almost overnight, the game seemed to find a popularity it had never enjoyed before. The reason for this, of course, was the arrival of Earvin "Magic" Johnson and Larry Bird.

Their college teams had met for the first time in the 1979 NCAA

championship game. Bird and Indiana State against Magic and Michigan State. The resulting battle attracted the highest television ratings in the history of the Final Four.

They were merely college athletes, each of them relatively unknown before that season, yet their chemistry was so strong it was nearly tangible. And practically inexplicable. Although major television networks have spent millions since then hyping and promoting the NCAA championship, the ratings have never equalled those of the 1979 game.

"It was as if this massive national television audience had a sixth sense for history," college basketball analyst Billy Packer said in amazement a decade afterward.

What the audience apparently

open with reporters and fans alike.

Larry Bird rested somewhere at the other end of the spectrum. He moved through his senior season at Indiana State with a grim silence. He didn't trust reporters and seldom spoke with them. The Sycamores were an unheralded team, and the burden of carrying them seemed to have left him sullen.

Only when his team had reached the NCAA championship game in Salt Lake City did Bird loosen up a bit. "To me, it's a serious game," he said when asked by reporters about the difference between Magic and himself. "Now you wouldn't expect me to be havin' all kinds of fun when the score's tied, two seconds are left on the clock and the other guys have the ball. It's nice that Magic laughs a lot. I just hope he won't be laughing in my face after he makes a big play."

Actually, Magic was pretty good about keeping his game face affixed. Only after the Spartans had defeated Indiana State for the national championship did he allow himself a smile. Then he went home, got some rest and began pondering his future. Should he turn professional? It was a big decision. His coaches and fans at Michigan State—even Jay Vincent, his childhood friend and college teammate—said he should stay in school.

Bird, on the other hand, already had his future set out for him. The Celtics had drafted him with the sixth pick of the first round the previous spring (1978). As a fifth-year college player, Bird had been eligible for the draft, and Boston was willing to give him a $650,000-per-year deal, then the highest salary ever paid an NBA rookie.

"Now, I don't think I'm worth as much as Bird," Magic said facetiously that spring as he waited to make his decision. "Let's be honest. He played longer, has got the experience and the accolades and, besides, wow, he's a white superstar. Basketball sure needs him. But think of me in the NBA. One thing I'm always going to do is have fun. There is time for business, time for school and time for fun. You know, things can be

But as a Laker, Kareem was frustrated until Magic arrived. (Koch photo)

happenin' at a party before I get there, but when I show up they just happen more."

Magic decided to join Larry Bird at the NBA party that fall of 1979, and just as he had predicted, things started happenin'. He made the rounds of the summer all-star games and rookie leagues, and everywhere he went, large crowds gathered. People were impressed with what they saw. It didn't take much of a scouting eye to know that something special had arrived in pro basketball.

In retrospect, the league can be ever so thankful that it did. Bird and Magic provided the juice for the NBA's resurgence. Over the next dozen years, the league's television rights money alone zoomed from roughly $14 million per year to more than $150 million. "There's no question that Bird and Magic

together, with the rivalry they brought us, was an important factor," said Russ Granick, the NBA's executive vice president.

THE MAGIC MAN

A sportswriter who followed his team in high school first gave him the nickname Magic.

Magic because of his beamer of a smile. Magic because of his uncanny ability with a basketball. But mostly he was Magic because he somehow transformed good teams into great ones.

He did that everywhere he played. At Everett High School in East Lansing, Michigan. At Michigan State. And finally in Los Angeles.

"I'm asked a lot what was the greatest thing Earvin did," Michigan State Coach Jud Heathcote said.

"Many say passing the ball, his great court sense, the fact that he could rebound. I say the greatest things Earvin did were intangible. He always made the guys he played with better. In summer pick-up games, Earvin would take three or four non-players, and he'd make those guys look so much better and they would win, not because he was making the baskets all by himself, but because he just made other players play better."

A 6'8", 220-pounder, he came to State after leading Everett High to the state title in the spring of 1977.

"I'd heard about him at Everett High School," Terry Donnelly, his teammate at Michigan State, recalled, "and I'd even seen him play. But it didn't really hit me until I got in the backcourt with him, on the first day of practice. You're running down the floor and you're open and most people can't get the ball to you through two or three people, but all of a sudden the ball's in your hands and you've got a layup."

To his credit, Heathcote immediately recognized Magic's unique talent. Although the Michigan State program was short on big men, the coach didn't hesitate to run Johnson at the point. "I still remember the first game that Earvin played," Heathcote said. "We were playing Central Michigan. I think he had seven points and about eight turnovers, and everyone said,

Magic took Michigan State to the 1979 NCAA championship. (Indiana State University photo)

'Heathcoate's crazy. He's got Earvin handling the ball in the break, he's got him playing guard out there on offense, he' s got him running the break, he's got him doing so many different things. Nobody can do all those things.' It's just that Earvin was nervous playing that first game and he didn't play like he played in practice. Actually, he was very comfortable in all those areas. When he went to the pros and right away they had him playing forward, I said sooner or later they'll realize that Earvin can play anywhere on defense and he has to have the ball on offense."

BUCK

The Los Angeles Lakers needed many things in the fall of 1979. They needed rebounding help for Kareem in the frontcourt, and as Heathcote projected, Magic filled in nicely as a power forward on the defensive end. The Lakers also needed help for Norm Nixon in the backcourt. And although Nixon was already a young, promising point guard, the Lakers moved Magic in to share the ball at the point.

Yet perhaps the team's biggest need as it opened the 1980s was enthusiasm. No one player needed this more than Kareem, who had

carried the Lakers for half a decade. During that time, the team had failed to reach the Finals, which meant the giant center was blamed for this shortcoming. The criticism had been particularly stinging when the Lakers were thumped by Seattle in the second round of the 1979 playoffs. "Is it fair?" Kareem replied when reporters asked about the situation. "Of course not. But I'm a target. Always have been. Too big to miss."

Some observers figured Kareem might have retired from basketball had Magic not come along to give him some help. Named Lew Alcindor before his conversion to Islam, Kareem had grown up in New York

Magic and Larry spiced up the NBA competition. (Soohoo photo)

Magic helped Kareem on the boards in the '82 Finals. (Koch photo)

take away the anguish of losing. Adbul-Jabbar's response to the circumstances was to pull even deeper within his shell. His already cool approach to the game became ever cooler.

Magic, of course, came along and changed all that.

"His enthusiasm was something out of this world," said Jamaal Wilkes, then the Lakers' small forward, "something I had never seen prior to him and something I haven't seen since. It just kind of gave everyone a shot in the arm."

For the 20-year-old Magic, life was one big joyful disco, a trip from one jam to another. All he had to do was pop on the headset, snap his fingers and smile. The team eventually took to calling him Young Buck, which was shortened to Buck, because of his zeal. When Kareem won their opening game at San Diego with one of his skyhooks, Magic smothered him in a youthful celebration. The big center was obviously startled. Take it easy, kid, he said. We've got 81 more of these to play.

"Everybody was shocked," Magic recalled, "but I was used to showing my emotions."

Reality did set in for the Lakers shortly thereafter. In fact, there were problems aplenty. But they couldn't dent Magic's boundless optimism that propelled him always in a positive direction.

First, there was the new coach. The Lakers had hired veteran assistant Jack McKinney, a guy fascinated by the running game, to run the team. McKinney promptly set up an offense geared to Magic's abilities, and he acquired Jim Chones, the veteran forward, to help Kareem up front. It worked

and become a legend at Power Memorial Academy. Projected as the second coming of Wilt Chamberlain, he bettered those prophesies by leading UCLA to three consecutive NCAA championships from 1967-69. John Wooden, his college coach, described him as the most valuable college basketball player ever, the kind of center around which a dynasty could be built. Kareem expanded on that reputation in the NBA when he teamed with Oscar Robertson to give the Milwaukee Bucks a world championship in 1971, the team's third season of operation. In 1974, he again led the Bucks to the Finals, where they lost to the Celtics in seven games. But Kareem wasn't particularly happy in Milwaukee. Most of his social life was centered in Los Angeles. And after the 1975 season,

the Bucks gave him his wish and traded him to the Lakers, which brought a string of four frustrating years of playoff failures.

With each playoff loss, the criticism grew louder. Insiders knew better, but Kareem was accused of having lost his drive. When the Portland Trail Blazers whipped the Lakers in the 1977 playoffs, some writers suggested that Portland center Bill Walton had outplayed Kareem. The Blazers, however, were sincere in their respect for the Lakers' center. "Jabbar would never give up," Portland forward Maurice Lucas said as the series ended. "He's the most respected player in the league because he never bows his head. Such great inner strength. You may beat his team but you never beat him."

The praise was good, but it didn't

Wilkes scores on the Doctor. (Koch photo)

beautifully. They opened the season 9-4 and were primed to scoot.

But then tragedy struck. McKinney suffered a serious head injury in a bicycle accident. He had beenheaded to a tennis match with his best friend and assistant coach, Paul Westhead. For a time, it appeared McKinney might not make it. At the very least, he faced months of convalescence. So Westhead, a Shakespearean scholar, served as interim coach, and the Lakers moved on.

Magic's presence certainly proved good for Kareem. The Lakers center won the league's MVP for an unprecedented sixth time (Russell had won five). "When you paint a picture," Westhead told the writers, "the sunshine goes in first, then you fill in the trees and the flowers."

Abdul-Jabbar was shining more

than ever in the Lakers' universe, the coach said. As a result, Los Angeles finished as the top team in the Western Conference with a 60-22 record.

Only Bird's Celtics bettered that with a 61-21 finish. The young forward had averaged 21.5 points in leading his team to what was then the best turnaround in league history. The year before Bird arrived, Boston had finished 29-53. That upswing of 32 games resulted in Bird being named rookie of the year.

And that, in turn, injected high octane into Magic's competitive carburetor. During the regular season he had averaged 17.6 points, 7.7 rebounds and 7.3 assists while shooting 52 percent from the floor. He upped those numbers during his 16 playoff games that spring of 1980 to

18.3 points, 10.5 rebounds and 9.4 assists.

With the team in synch and Kareem playing his best ball in years, the Lakers ditched Phoenix and defending champion Seattle on their way to the Western Conference championship and the Finals.

Bird's Celtics, meanwhile, had run aground against Julius Erving and the Philadelphia 76ers in the Eastern Conference finals and lost 4-1. The 'Sixers, coached by Billy Cunningham, had finished 59-23, just two games behind Boston during the regular season. They brought a strong, veteran lineup to face the Lakers for the 1980 title. Erving was still at the top of his high-flying game. "I don't think about my dunk shots," he had said during the Boston series. "I just make sure I have a place to land."

The 6'11" Darryl Dawkins joined 7'1" Caldwell Jones in the Philly frontcourt. The sixth man was Bobby Jones, and the 'Sixers also got good minutes and 11.6 points from veteran Steve Mix. The guards were Maurice Cheeks, Henry Bibby and Lionel Hollins.

The matchup of Caldwell Jones and Dawkins against Kareem was particularly intriguing. The Lakers center claimed the first round for himself and his team with 33 points, 14 rebounds, six blocks and five assists on the way to a 109-102 win in the Forum. For the first time in years, though, Kareem didn't have to go it alone for Los Angeles. Nixon had 23 points and Wilkes finished with 20 while doing an excellent double-team job on Erving. "Every time I caught the ball I had two people on me," the Philly star said afterward.

Magic, too, lived up to his game with 16 points, nine assists and 10 rebounds. More and more in the playoffs, Westhead went to Magic as the power forward on offense, while Nixon and sixth-man Michael Cooper ran the backcourt.

"That's our best lineup," the coach said.

Dawkins had opened the series with a rumble of a dunk from his

Chocolate Thunder but soon saw his storm melt away in the face of Kareem's sunshine. The Sixers' center finished with a mere 12 points, three rebounds, and a passel of offensive fouls and turnovers. "I ain't afraid to go to the hoop on Kareem," Dawkins allowed afterward. "But when the refs are callin' 'em that way, it's a waste of time. I lost my funk."

Despite their 1-0 lead, the Lakers encountered a personnel distraction just as they were trying to win the title. Veteran Spencer Haywood fell asleep during during stretching exercises before Game Two. Haywood, once a superstar and now a reserve, had been disgruntled most of the season. His attitude led to a flareup with his teammates after the game, and Westhead suspended him, which left the Lakers' thin in the frontcourt.

In the middle of this distraction, the Lakers dropped Game Two, 107-104, and the series was tied at one game apiece. Even worse, the Sixers had taken the homecourt advantage.

Los Angeles, however, quickly took in back. For Game Three, Westhead made a defensive switch, moving Chones to cover Dawkins. With only the non-shooting Caldwell Jones to worry about, Kareem parked his big frame in the lane and dared the Sixers to drive in. Westhead also shifted Magic to covering Lionel Hollins on the perimeter, which stifled Philly's outside game. The result of this double shutdown was a 111-101

Westhead and Riley on the bench.

More and more in the playoffs, Westhead went to Magic as the power forward on offense, while Nixon and sixth-man Michael Cooper ran the backcourt.

L.A. win and a 2-1 lead. The Lakers' big guy had again put up big numbers—33 points, 14 rebounds, four blocks and three assists. And once again he got plenty of help from Nixon, Johnson and Wilkes.

As expected, Philly lashed back for Game Four.

The lead switched back and forth through the first three periods, then the Sixers took control in the fourth. That, for those with a hearty memory, was when the Doctor unleashed one of his more memorable moves, scooting around Laker reserve Mark Landsberger on the right to launch himself. In midair, headed toward the hoop, Erving encountered Kareem. Somehow the Doctor moved behind the backboard and freed his right arm behind Kareem to put it in. It was pure magic—the Philly variety, and the Sixers went on to even the series at 2-all with a 105-102 win.

All of which set up a Fabulous Game Five back at the Forum. Los Angeles clutched to a two-point lead late in the third quarter when Kareem

With Magic's arrival, Norm Nixon moved to off guard.

twisted his left ankle and went to the locker room. At that point, he had 26 points and was carrying the Lakers despite an uneven performance from Magic. But the rookie took over with the team captain out. He scored six points and added an assist as Los Angeles moved up by eight.

That was enough to buy time for Adbul-Jabbar, who limped back into the game early in the fourth period. His appearance aroused the Forum regulars to a roar, and despite the bad ankle, he acknowledged their support by scoring 14 points down the stretch. With the game tied at 103 and 33 seconds left, Kareem scored, drew the foul and finished Philly by completing the three-point play. Los Angeles won, 108-103, and took the series lead, 3-2.

The Lakers arrived at Los Angeles International Airport for their flight to Philly that next morning, Thursday May 15, and learned that Kareem wouldn't be making the trip. His ankle was so bad, doctors told him to stay home and try to get ready for Game Seven.

Westhead was worried about the effect the news would have on the team. In a private meeting, the coach told Magic he would have to move to center. No problem, the young guard replied. He had played center in high school and loved just this kind of challenge.

When the team boarded its United Airlines flight to Philadelphia, Magic plopped himself down in the first-class seat always set aside for Abdul-Jabbar. Then he went through Kareem's normal routine, stretching out in the seat and pulling a flight blanket over his head. This done, Magic looked back at his coach and winked.

"Never fear," he told his teammates. "E.J. is here."

Somehow the folks in Philly never really believed the Lakers would head into the game without their captain. Radio stations reported regular sightings of Kareem at the airport. One taxi driver even claimed to have taken the center to his hotel.

Cunningham was just as distrusting as the man on the street.

"I'll believe he's not coming when the game ends and I haven't seen him," the coach told the writers.

Westhead, meanwhile, feared the Lakers were too loose. Magic was his normal jammin', dancin' self. About the only thing that punctured his mood were reporters' questions about his thoughts for Game Seven. It was

Paul Westhead.

perfect, he told his teammates. Nobody expects us to win here. In reality, most of the Lakers figured they didn't have a chance either.

But when they arrived at the Spectrum that Friday evening, they were greeted by the sounds of carpenters hammering out an awards presentation platform. The NBA rules required that Philadelphia provide some facility to present the trophy, just in case Los Angeles happened to win.

"It should be interesting," Westhead told his players before the game. "Pure democracy. We'll go with the slim line."

Which meant Magic, Chones and Wilkes in the frontcourt while Nixon and Cooper took care of things up top. Kareem, who was sprawled on his bed back at his Bel-Air home, sent a last-minute message.

Go for it.

With that last blast pushing them sky high, the Lakers took the floor.

Magic grinned broadly as he stepped up to jump center. The Sixers seemed puzzled. Los Angeles went up 7-0, then 11-4. Finally Philly broke back in the second quarter and took a 52-44 lead. Westhead stopped play and told his guys to collapse more in the middle. The Lakers listened and closed to 60-all at the half.

Then they opened the third period with a 14-0 run, keyed by Wilkes. But the Sixers drew close again in the fourth.

Back home in Bel-Air, Kareem was twisting and turning and going crazy watching the television from his bed. Finally, late in the last period, he got up and hobbled out to his back yard to let out a scream.

With a little over five minutes left, it was 103-101, Lakers. Westhead called time again and made one last attempt to charge up his tired players. They responded with a run over the next 76 seconds to go up by seven. Then Magic scored nine points down the stretch to end it, 123-107.

Across the roster, the Lakers had something to celebrate. Wilkes had a career-best outing, scoring 37 points with 10 rebounds. And Chones lived up to his vow to shut down the middle. He finished with 11 points and 10 rebounds and held Dawkins to another Chocolate Blunder type of game, 14 points and four rebounds.

For the Lakers, even Landsberger had 10 boards. And Cooper put in 16 points.

But the big news, of course, was Magic, who simply was. He scored 42, including all 14 of his free throw attempts. He had 15 rebounds, seven assists, three steals and a block.

"It was amazing, just amazing," said Erving, who led Philly with 27.

"Magic was outstanding. Unreal," agreed injured Philly guard Doug Collins. "I knew he was good but I never realized he was great."

He was the hands-down choice as series MVP. "What position did I play?" Magic replied for the reporters afterward. "Well, I played center, a little forward, some guard. I tried to think up a name for it, but the best I could come up with was CFG-Rover."

How had they done it without their

center? Magic was asked. "Without Kareem," he said, "we couldn't play the halfcourt and think defensively. We had to play the full court and take our chances."

Then in the post-game interview on national television, Magic turned to the camera and addressed Kareem back home. "We know you're hurtin' Big Fella," he said. "But we want you to get up and do a little dancin' tonight."

The Lakers partied all the way back to Los Angeles, where Kareem and a cast of thousands greeted them at the airport. There were hugs and cheers and high fives all around.

E.J. the deejay had delivered. Again. "You can't compare this one with winning the NCAA at Michigan State," he said. "That was great, but this is the one. This is professional. This is better."

TROUBLES

Things turned bad shortly thereafter. The 1981 season soon became as frustrating as '80 had been satisfying. Magic suffered a cartilege tear in his knee during the season, then struggled back from surgery to rejoin his team late in the schedule. But they didn't have time to jell and lost to Moses Malone and a plodding Houston Rockets team, 2-1, in the opening round of the playoffs.

The Lakers regrouped for the next season, but their list of troubles was long and substantial:

* Just weeks before training camp opened, Jamaal Wilkes lost his second infant daughter to crib death (his first daughter had died of heart disease);

* In mid November, the team struggled offensively. Discontent grew among the players, and finally the Lakers decided to release Westhead. In announcing a coaching change, Jerry Buss complimented Westhead but said circumstances required somebody new;

* The team was then caught in confusion over the identity of the head coach. Buss had badly wanted Jerry West, then a personnel consultant to the team, to return to the bench. West, who had coached the Lakers from 1976-79, vehemently declined and instead offered to help

Westhead and Buss get the '80 trophy as Brent Musberger of CBS and Wilkes join in the fun.

36-year-old assistant coach Pat Riley adjust to being the team's boss;

* In December, power forward Mitch Kupchak, the Lakers' new high-priced free agent, blew his knee out in a game at San Diego and was lost for the season;

* Just days after Kupchak went down, Kareem suffered a severe ankle sprain;

The injuries left the Lakers decimated in the frontcourt. Faced with this adversity, the team responded by going on a short winning streak, much of it coming from Earvin's emotion. But it was clear that enthusiasm could only carry them so far. Even when Kareem returned they would face the same dearth of rebounding.

But then help arrived in two very unexpected forms. First came the acquisition of 30-year-old free agent Robert McAdoo, the same McAdoo who was disdained in Boston and considered a selfish problem in Detroit, who had a league MVP award and two scoring titles under his belt. Few people figured he would fit in with the Lakers, but he showed a remarkable willingness to play off the bench. Even better, he was good at it, giving the team just the scoring punch it needed at key times.

The other unexpected aid came with the emergence of power forward Kurt Rambis, the Clark Kent lookalike and free agent who reluctantly signed with the Lakers only after management assured him he had a solid shot at making the team. Not long after Kupchak went down, Rambis got an unexpected start and responded with 14 rebounds. He couldn't shoot and had a noticeable lack of athleticism. But the Lakers had enough of those properties. They needed his hustle, his defense, his rebounding, and his physical play. Combined with the other Showtime elements and Kareem's return, McAdoo and Rambis would became a major factor in the team's playoff success.

But before that happened, there was more rough terrain to cross. The Lakers struggled through a couple of short losing streaks in January, and Riley seemed a bit lost. The son of a

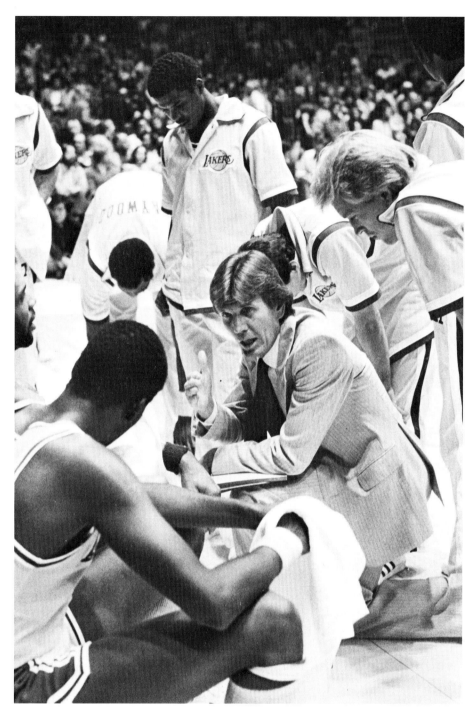

Westhead talks during a timeout. (Laker photo)

minor league baseball manager, he had starred in football, basketball and baseball in high school in New Jersey. Bear Bryant had wanted him as a quarterback for the University of Alabama, but Riley decided to play basketball for Adolph Rupp at the University of Kentucky. There, he had been an All-American forward in the 1960s and had starred on Rupp's last Final Four team in 1965. He was a first-round draft pick of the San Diego Rockets, but in the pros, his transition to guard was difficult. He spent most of his seven-year career as a backup, although he was a solid contributor on the Lakers 1972 championship team. After his playing days he wound up serving as the color analyst on Laker radio broadcasts with Chick Hearn. Riley was working that spot in the fall of 1979 when Westhead had asked him to be an assistant coach. Riley jumped at the chance and remained loyal, even after Westhead was fired.

The Lakers met the Sixers in the Finals three times in four years. (Bernstein photo)

Pat Riley took over in 1981. (Bernstein photo)

"I was numb," Riley said. "I thought the firing was horrible."

Although confused, he agreed to take the head job, and he agreed to make the wide-open, full-speed game the team's top option, which meant that Magic was smiling and juking and jamming once again. But the return of Showtime basketball still didn't translate into immediate success. Between January and March, the Lakers barely played .500 ball.

"Don't be afraid to coach the team," Jerry Buss finally told Riley in one meeting.

"I was giving the players too much responsiblity," Riley explained later.

He began to assert himself. When the team lost at home to Chicago on March 12, he flashed his anger. "I got fed up," he said. "I didn't know what I wanted to do when I took the job. I looked at the players, and I respected their games so much, and I respected them as people. I gave them too much trust. I said, 'This is their team.' It was their team, but they needed direction. That's my job. It took me three months to realize it, but I have

certain responsibilities to push and demand. They have to play. I have to coach. They were waiting for me to put my foot down. That's my nature anyhow."

He put his foot down, and no one shouted. In fact, the players seemed relieved. Despite their struggles, they finished the regular season with a best-in-the-West 57-25 record. But more important, they were peaking as the playoffs opened. After March 31, they won 21 of their final 24 games. Suddenly Buss raised his eyebrows. His second choice as coach was getting the job done.

Much of the success, of course, was due to Magic, who fought through the distraction of the booing by concentrating on his game. "The crowds still get me going," Magic said toward the end of the regular schedule. "They still jack me up. And I still love the game. I don't think I'll ever lose that."

"Magic has become a great player," Jerry West told the writers. "I've watched him go from one level to another, higher level this year. He's become solid, that's the big

thing. He's in control out there. He knows what he's doing every minute he's on the floor. He's had a great, great season, especially under the circumstances."

The Doc and Philadelphia whipped the Celtics to win the Eastern Conference, and the Lakers dispatched Phoenix and San Antonio, 4-0 each, to meet Philly in the Finals. The appearance of the two clubs wasn't so much a clash as it was a mixing of glitter and style. These were two elegant basketball teams that shared several common properties, none of which was more prominent than the sense of embarrassment they had suffered in the 1981 playoffs. While the Lakers were falling to Houston in the first round, the Sixers had folded meekly in the Eastern finals after leading the Boston Celtics, 3-1.

Riley acknowledged this common embarrassment as the 1982 Finals opened. "When I looked at the entire playoff picture," he told the writers, "I thought the two teams most committed to winning this year would be the two teams that were stung and

Nixon challenges the Sixers. (Laker photo)

humiliated last year. Philadelphia, I felt, was the best team last year, but they gave it away. That was the ultimate slap in the face. Then there was our humiliating loss, and our players remember that pain. Maturity makes the veterans ask, 'How many more times are we going to have the chance to win it with Kareem or with

"I've always been his fan," Johnson said of the Doctor. "I respect him. I'm in awe of him. But when you've got a job to do, you do it the best you can."

Doc?' I see that with this team, and it could be a tremendous motivating force. They talk about it constantly."

Riley's intuition proved correct. If nothing else, the Lakers and Sixers were motivated. After all, time was running down on their opportunity for greatness. For Philly, there was the Doctor, Julius Erving, a poetic player if there ever was one, with his acrobatic moves to the basket, his twirling dunks, his well-spoken, diplomatic manner. But he was 32 as the 1982 playoffs opened, and he was making his third trip to the Finals since coming to the NBA from the American Basketball Association in 1976. Each time the Sixers failed, they had to fight the public perception that they were wasting Erving's bountiful talent.

Kareem, too, was thinking about age. He had turned 35 during the season, and with each year speculation had increased about his impending retirement. It helped, of course, that he now played with the 22-year-old Magic, if not a fountain of youth, certainly a spring of enthusiasm. In 1982, it would have seemed unimaginable that Magic's presence could keep the great Laker center playing another seven years. By no means would those seasons be easy or uncomplicated. Still, they would be fruitful, bringing the Lakers

Magic rejuvenated the Cap. (Bernstein photo)

three more titles. And if that didn't keep Abdul-Jabbar young, it at least made him ageless.

And seemingly tireless.

"That's the best thing about this team," Riley said. "The work ethic."

The second best thing was their nifty zone trap. They produced it at just the right time in the opener at the Spectrum on Thursday May 27. Fresh from the battle of Boston, the Sixers worked their offense to precision until midway through the third period. At the time, Philadelphia led by 15. Then over the next 11 minutes or so, the Lakers ripped through a 40-9 blitz. The bewildered Sixers fell, 124-117, and that quickly the Lakers had snatched away the home-court advantage.

But Riley then changed gears for

Game Two, deciding to back off the trap a bit. Instead, he switched Magic to cover Erving on defense. "Magic on Doc seemed like an ideal matchup to me," Riley said. "Dr. J. is a great offensive rebounder. He'd hurt us real bad. Defensive rebounding, that's Magic's greatest strength. So we put him in the position we wanted him to be in. It was great to watch. No pushing, no shoving, no hammering. They played with their talents. Magic played him as honestly as he could play him. Two great players going against each other."

"I've always been his fan," Johnson said of the Doctor. "I respect him. I'm in awe of him. But when you've got a job to do, you do it the best you can."

For Game Two, that wasn't quite

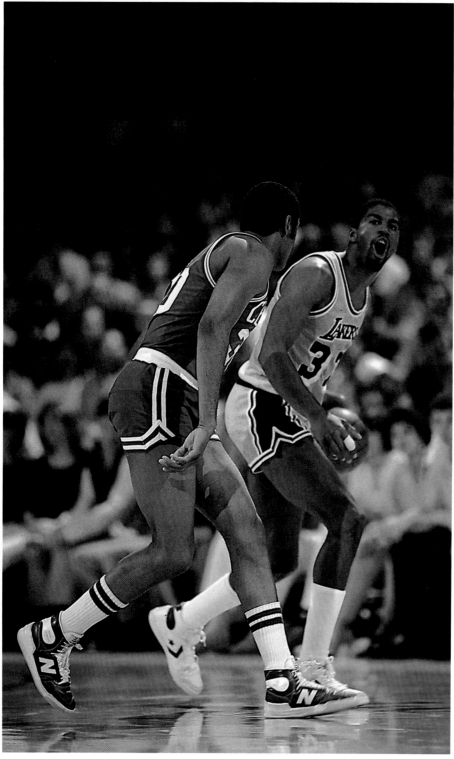

Earvin learned tough lessons in the '84 Finals. (Bernstein photo)

"Tonight was just a bad game for us," Caldwell Jones offered lamely.

So was the next night, Thursday June 3. The Lakers controlled the series by ditching Showtime and going to their half-court power game with Kareem. On the other end, they kept up the pressure with their zone trap. All together, it was enough for a first-half run that put the contest away. The Lakers went up, 3-1, with a 111-101 win. Wilkes and Magic had 24 each, while Kareen added 22 and McAdoo 19. Rambis thumped his way to 11 rebounds.

"We haven't won it yet, but we're starting to smell the aroma," Riley told the writers.

Unfortunately, something was rotten in Philly. The Sixers reverted to their old power for Game Five. In a shocker, they held Kareem to just six points. He hadn't scored that few since being tossed out of a game for punching out Kent Benson a few years earlier.

"They pushed and shoved a lot," Abdul-Jabbar explained in a quote memo handed out to the writers. The Lakers center departed the locker room before speaking personally with the media.

Playing one of the better defensive games in his career, Dawkins had been the prime pusher and shover. "I tried working hard," Chocolate Thunder said. "I tried stopping him from getting position. It's hard. He's strong, and if you let him get position he gets the skyhook. You can't block that. Wilt Chamberlain couldn't block it, so how do you expect me to block it?"

Their strong showing gave the Sixers hope as they headed cross country for Game Six in the Forum. But again Philadelphia failed to come up with a team effort. Erving scored 30 and Toney 29, but Dawkins got six fouls, one rebound and 10 points in only 20 minutes of play. Everyone else struggled.

The Lakers got the lead early and were up, 66-57, at the half. Finally, in the third period, the Sixers found some defensive toughness. They held Los Angeles to 20 points for the

good enough as Erving brought the Sixers back with 24 points and 16 rebounds. Cunningham ran all three of his centers—Caldwell Jones, Darryl Dawkins and Earl Cureton—at Kareem. It worked. The Sixers took a 110-94 win that evened the series at 1-all.

Philly, though, enjoyed only a brief respite. The Lakers dominated the next two games in the Forum. Norm Nixon led a parade in Game Three with 29, and the Lakers marched, 129-108. Again the zone trap was Philly's undoing. But the Sixers did their share, too, with incredibly flat play. Andrew Toney scored 36 and Erving 21, but no one else showed up.

quarter and several times cut the lead to one.

"I had a few butterflies about then," said Wilkes, who led six Lakers in double figures with 27.

But the Lakers surged to boost their lead to 11 early in the fourth period. Toney and the Doctor responded, and with a little under four minutes to go trimmed the edge to 103-100.

That was about as far as the pair could take Philadelphia, however. Kareem scored and was fouled on the next play. He made the free throw to put Los Angeles up by six. Moments later, Wilkes got a breakaway layup to close it out, 114-104.

The Lakers had won yet another title with yet another rookie coach. Riley and Buss smiled broadly as the Lakers owner accepted the trophy afterward. "It seems like a millenium since I took over," Riley said of seven months as a head coach. "Yeah, a millenium. I've got brain drain right now, mush brain. I dug down for everything I could find. I need four months to rest up."

Johnson with 13 points, 13 rebounds and 13 assists in Game 6 was named the series MVP, an award that some writers found controversial.

The Lakers, though, had had about all the controversy they could stand for one season. "There were times earlier in the year when I didn't think this would be possible," Wilkes said as champagne cascaded over his face. "We had so many unhappy people around here you wouldn't believe it."

Of the newly happy faces, none was happier than McAdoo, who had 16 points, nine rebounds and three blocks in Game Six. Throughout the series, he had provided consistent scoring and rebounding off the bench. "This is the happiest moment of my life," he said. "People have said bad things about me during my career, but this makes up for it. I always said I would trade my scoring titles to be on a championship team, but I guess that wasn't necessary."

Once again, the Sixers had been

left to answer the tough questions. After three trips to the Finals, Erving still had no NBA title ring. "My heart really goes out to him," Wilkes said. "He's a basketball genius and a complete gentleman, and I love him. I would have loved for him to get a championship ring, but not at our expense."

Yet that is exactly what would happen down the road. Erving would get his championship, and the Lakers would pick up the tab. Philly team owner Harold Katz aquired Moses Malone from Houston for the 1982-83 season, and the Sixers swept the limping Lakers in the Finals, 4-0.

BATTLING BOSTON

For four seasons, they had danced around each other in the NBA, meeting only twice each year in regular-season games. Still, Larry and Magic were always aware of each other. They searched the headlines and kept their eyes on the standings and the box scores. Finally, in 1984, they met for the championship.

Lakers vs. Celtics.

Across America, it was portrayed as a clash of symbols. East vs. West. Tradition vs. New Wave. Hollywood vs. Beantown. Showtime vs.

Wilkes scores in the Garden during the '84 Finals. (Bernstein photo)

39

> **"What will I remember most from this series? Simple. Game Two. Worthy's pass to Scott. I could see the seams of the ball, like it was spinning in slow motion, but I couldn't do anything about it."**
>
> **—Pat Riley**

Kupchak came back from a knee injury to help out in the frontcourt. (Laker photo)

Shamrocks. Celtic Pride vs. L.A. Cool.

"It's like the opening of a great play," Lakers General Manager Jerry West told the writers just before the 1984 Finals. "Everyone's waiting to see it."

The media hype was tremendous. But beneath all the symbols and media, at the heart of everything, were two guys with immense confidence, supreme talent, and a mutual desire to dominate.

"With Magic, it's a macho thing," West explained in 1990. "He wants to be better than everybody else."

The same was true with Bird. "The number one thing is desire," he said, "the ability to do the things you have to do to become a basketball player. I don't think you can teach anyone desire. I think it's a gift. I don't know why I have it, but I do."

As Magic once explained, "I only know how to play two ways. That's reckless and abandon."

And that's how they approached their 1984 championship bash. Reckless and abandon. Two forces of pride and ego colliding.

Both teams had been through some changes. Boston had added K.C. Jones as head coach and aquired Dennis Johnson at guard. After the Lakers were swept by Philadelphia in the 1983 Finals, Jerry West spent his nights figuring ways for a quick reshuffle. Finally during the 1983-84 preseason, he sent starting guard Norm Nixon and reserve Eddie Jordan to the San Diego Clippers for backup center

Swen Nater and the draft rights to rookie guard Byron Scott, out of Arizona State. In short time, the 6'4" Scott would work right in to the Laker backcourt, and Showtime would be off and running again.

With injuries and other problems, they finished the regular season at 54-28. Magic had missed 13 games early in the schedule with an injured finger. Then in February, Jamaal Wilkes contracted an intestinal infection that hampered him the remainder of the season. Still, the year held its special moments. Kareem had first broken Chamberlain's record for career field goals, then for career scoring when he picked up his 36,420th point against the Utah Jazz. Although he was no longer as dominant as he had once been, Kareem still gave the Lakers a formidable half-court game when they needed it.

Beyond that, James Worthy had quietly come into his own as a forward. He had brilliant quickness, and once Magic got him the ball in

the low post, the result was usually a score. He took delight in faking one way then exploding another. And he continued to add range to his shot, building his consistency from 15 feet out.

The Lakers also continued to get good frontcourt minutes and scoring from McAdoo. In the backcourt, Michael Cooper had found his identity as a defensive and three-point specialist, while third-year guard Mike McGee contributed 9.8 points per game.

Once Magic put his finger injury behind him, they zipped to a strong finish, including a nice little roll through the early rounds of the playoffs. As the Finals opened, there was a sense that Los Angeles was the better team. K.C. Jones said nearly as much. "The Lakers are more talented than we are," he concluded in an obvious attempt to get any psychological advantage possible.

The Boston advantage was thought to be rest and the homecourt. The Celtics had ended their conference finals series on May 23, while the Lakers didn't wrap things up until Friday night May 25. With the first game of the Finals set for Sunday May 27 in Boston Garden, the Celtics' four days rest seemed to be a major factor.

From the Laker perspective, the situation was laced with tension. It had been 15 years since Los Angeles had last faced Boston in the Finals, yet the numbers were on everyone's mind. Seven times the Lakers had met the Celtics for the championship, and seven times the Lakers had lost.

Hours before Game One, Kareem was wracked by one of the migraine headaches that had troubled him throughout his career. Team trainer Jack Curran worked the center's neck and back an hour before game time, at one point popping a vetebrae into place. That seemed to do the trick on the 37-year-old captain. He walked out and treated the Garden crowd to 32 points, eight rebounds, five assists, two blocks and a steal. He made 12 of his 17 shots from the floor and eight of nine free throws. He did all of that only when the Lakers slowed down. They spent the rest of the time running their break in one door and out another for a 115-109 win.

Kaput went Boston's home-court edge.

Game Two then became a Worthy showcase for the first 47 minutes or so. He hit 11 of 12 from the floor and scored 29 points. Even better, the Lakers had come from behind to take a 115-113 lead with 18 seconds left. McHale went to the free throw line for two shots but missed both. Yet just when the crowd was thinking about the possibility of a sweep, the Lakers picked that particular moment for a snooze. Inbounding at mid court, Magic tossed the ball to Worthy, who spied Byron Scott across the court and attempted to get the ball to him. Lurking in the background praying for just such an opportunity was Boston guard Gerald Henderson. He stepped in, snatched the fat pass and loped down the court for the layin. The game was tied, but again Magic made a mistake. He allowed the clock to run down without attempting a final shot.

"The other players never did anything to help him," Riley would say later in defense of Magic. "They stood out on the perimeter and didn't get open. Kareem moved with 12 seconds left, which meant he was open too early. Magic got blamed."

Late in overtime, Henderson found Wedman on the baseline and got him the ball. From there, the reserve forward put down the key jumper to give Boston a 124-121 win and a 1-1 tie in the series.

Afterward, Riley could only think about Henderson's steal. "What will I remember most from this series?" he asked rhetorically. "Simple. Game Two. Worthy's pass to Scott. I could see the seams of the ball, like it was spinning in slow motion, but I couldn't do anything about it."

However deep their disappointment, the Lakers quickly recovered back home in the Forum. Magic had a Finals record 21 assists, and Showtime rolled to a 137-104 win. Bird was outraged at Boston's flat performance. "We played like a bunch of sissies," he said.

The next day the Los Angeles papers began touting Worthy as the series MVP, a development that infuriated the Boston players. Jones

Worthy lit up Game Two in 1984. (Al Gonzalez photo)

The '85 Finals were all Showtime.

Riley drives home a point in the Garden. (Bernstein

adjusted the team's defense, switching D.J. to cover Magic, and they went back at it. The Lakers took an early lead and seemed poised to again run off with the game. From the bench, M.L. Carr vociferously lobbied for the Celtics to become more physical. McHale complied in the second quarter when he clotheslined Kurt Rambis on a breakaway, causing a ruckus under the basket. The incident awakened the Celtics and gave the Lakers reason to pause.

Later Riley would call the Celtics "a bunch of thugs."

Cedric Maxwell, on the other hand, was overjoyed with the development. "Before Kevin McHale hit Kurt Rambis, the Lakers were just running across the street whenever they wanted," he said. "Now they stop at the corner, push the button, wait for the light and look both ways."

Los Angeles had held a five-point lead with less than a minute to play in regulation. But Parish stole a bad pass from Magic, and the Laker point guard later missed two key free throws, allowing the Celtics to force an overtime. Late in the extra period, Worthy faced a key free throw. But Carr hooted loudly from the bench that he would miss. Worthy did, and Maxwell stepped up and greeted him with the choke sign. The Celtics vaulted to a 129-125 win to tie the series again and regain the homecourt edge.

The free throw misses and the turnover would trouble Magic for a long time. "I thought the free throws more than the pass were mistakes," he would say later. "Those were things I—not the team—I should have taken care of. When you miss the shots you go home and sit in the dark."

The Celtics realized they were on to something. The Lakers could be intimidated. "We had to go out and make some things happen," Henderson recalled of Game Four. "If being physical was gonna do it, then we had to do it. I remember in the fourth game that was the turnaround. We had to have that game or we were gonna be down 3-1."

Game Five back in Boston was the

The Celtic spell was broken in '85.

Kareem looks over the defense. (Bernstein photos)

crucial match. The heat in the Garden drained the Lakers, while Bird hit 15 for 20 from the floor for 34 points. The Celtics won, 121-103. Kareem, meanwhile, had appeared to be just what he was—a 37-year-old man running in sweltering heat. How hot was it? a reporter asked.

"I suggest," Kareem replied, "that you go to a local steam bath, do 100 pushups with all your clothes on, and then try to run back and forth for 48 minutes. The game was in slow motion. It was like we were running in mud."

"I love to play in the heat," Bird said, smiling. "I just run faster, create my own wind."

The Lakers then answered the Celtics' aggressiveness in Game Six back in the air-conditioned Forum. In the first period, Worthy shoved Maxwell into a basket support. From there, the Lakers rode their newfound toughness and an old standby. Kareem scored 30, and Los Angeles pulled away down the stretch for a 119-108 win to tie the series at three apiece. With that, they jetted back east to decide the seventh game.

The entire city of Boston was juiced up for the event that Tuesday night June 12. The Lakers needed a police escort to get from their hotel to North Station, the subway station that adjoins the Garden. Carr came out wearing goggles to mock Kareem and told the Lakers they weren't going to win. Not in the Garden.

Maxwell presented a high-action low-post puzzle that the Lakers never solved. He demoralized them on the offensive boards. He drew fouls. By halftime, he had made 11 of 13 free throws. When they tried to double-team him, he passed them silly. He finished with 24 points, eight assists and eight rebounds. Bird had 20 points and 12 rebounds, Parish 14 points and 16 rebounds.

Even against that barrage, the Lakers fought back from a 14-point deficit to trail by just three with more than a minute left. Magic had the ball, but Dennis Johnson knocked it loose. Coop recovered it for L.A. Magic again went to work and spied Worthy open under the basket. But before

Wilkes was smooth in offense, tough on defense. (Laker photo)

Magic could make the pass, Maxwell knocked the ball away yet again. Later the vision of Worthy open under the basket would return to Magic again and again.

At the other end, Dennis Johnson drew a foul and made the shots, spurring the Celtics to their fifteenth championship, 111-102.

Auerbach enjoyed yet another of his very fat, very special cigars as Commissioner David Stern presented the league trophy. The Celtics president clutched it with satisfaction and asked, "What ever happened to that Laker dynasty I've been hearing so much about?"

Unfortunately, the Lakers couldn't get out of town immediately after the 1984 Finals. Due to flight schedules, they had to spend one more night in their hotel, trapped inside of Boston with the Celtic blues again. Needless to say it was a sleepless night. Jerry Buss chainsmoked. Coop spent the

time in deep and miserable mourning sequestered in his room with his wife Wanda. Pat Riley just wished he had a reason to diagram tomorrow's plays, anything to fight the insomnia.

Magic was joined by his two friends, Isiah Thomas of the Detroit Pistons and Mark Aguirre of the Dallas Mavericks. They talked the night away. About music. Cars. Old times. Anything but the series. Occasionally the conversation would drift that way, but they'd steer it away. It was too tender a subject.

"We talked until the morning came," Thomas said later, "but we never talked about the game much. For that one night I think I was his escape from reality."

The pain would remain for months. Magic returned to California, where he was set to move into his new Bel-Air mansion, only the furniture hadn't arrived. His palace sat as empty as his heart. So he hid out for three days in his Culver City apartment. His mother, Christine, phoned to see how he was doing. He told her he just couldn't talk about it.

Yet everywhere he turned, there seemed to be something to read about it. The Celtics were having fun with their victory. McHale even dubbed him "Tragic Johnson." Asked about the 1984-85 season, Bird said of the Lakers, "I'd like to give them the opportunity to redeem themselves. I'm sure they have guys who feel they didn't play up to their capabilities." Asked if he meant Magic, Bird replied, "You think we don't love it? Magic having nightmares [about his poor play]."

Magic retorted that he had no need for redemption.

Even worse than the Celtic cockiness was the trashing he took from the L.A. newspapers. "I sat back when it was over," he said later, "and I thought, 'Man, did we just lose one of the great playoff series of all time, or didn't we?' This was one of the greatest in history. Yet all you read was how bad I was."

The Lakers answered with a fierceness that next season. By playoff time, the frontcourt was bolstered by the return of Mitch Kupchak and Jamaal Wilkes to go with Kareem, Worthy, Rambis, McAdoo and Larry Spriggs. The backcourt showed Magic, Scott, Coop and McGee. As a group, the Lakers were driven by their '84 humiliation.

"Those wounds from last June stayed open all summer," Riley said as the playoffs neared. "Now the misery has subsided, but it never leaves your mind completely. Magic is very sensitive to what people think about him, and in his own mind I think he heard those questions over and over again to the point where he began to rationalize and say, 'Maybe I do have to concentrate more.' I think the whole experience has made him grow up in a lot of ways."

After all, Johnson was a mere 25, and at a time when most pro players were just beginning to feel comfortable in the game, he already owned two championship rings. Across pro basketball, observers

The '86 playoff loss was stimulating, Riley said.

sensed that he was about to add to his jewelry collection. The Celtics, however, were conceding nothing. With a 63-19 regular-season finish, they had again claimed the home-court advantage. The Lakers had finished 62-20. And neither team dallied in the playoffs. Boston dismissed Cleveland, Detroit and Philadelphia in quick succession. The Lakers rolled past Phoenix, Portland and Denver.

For the first time in years, the Finals returned to a 2-3-2 format, with the first two games in Boston, the middle three in Los Angeles, and the last two, if necessary, back in Boston. The situation set up an immense opportunity for the Lakers to steal one

in the Garden, then pressure the Celtics back in Los Angeles. However it would be done, Magic, Kareem and company figured on rectifying their humiliation from 1984.

Little did they know they would have to suffer one final, profound embarrassment. Game One opened on Memorial Day, Monday May 27, with both teams cruising on five days rest. The Lakers, however, quickly took on the appearance of guys who had just come off two weeks on the graveyard shift. The 38-year-old Kareem, in particular, slogged up and down the court, while Robert Parish seemed to glide. Often Kareem would just be reaching the top of the key to catch up, when all of a sudden the

Riley with the goods from '85. (Bernstein photo)

action raced the other way. He finished the day with 12 points and three rebounds. And Magic had only one rebound. Meanwhile, the famed Showtime running game had been slowed to a belly crawl.

And the Celtics?

They placed a huge red welt on the Lakers' scar from the previous year, 148-114. Scott Wedman hit 11 for 11 from the floor, including four thee-pointers. But it was Danny Ainge who had lashed the whip, lacing in six straight buckets at the end of the first quarter to finish the period with 15 points. "It was one of those days," K.C. Jones said, "where if you turn around and close your eyes, the ball's gonna go in."

For all their success, the Celtics suddenly quieted their trash talking, as if they sensed that they had gone too far. They hadn't expected it to be this easy. And the last thing they wanted to do was rile the Lakers. "It's definitely time to back off," Maxwell said. "It's not like backgammon or cribbage, where if you beat someone bad enough you get two wins."

But it was too late. The teams didn't play again until Thursday, and there was an uneasy air in Boston despite the big win.

The next morning in the Lakers' film sessions, Kareem moved to the front row, rather than recline in the farther reaches as he usually did. And he didn't blink when Riley ran and reran the gruesome evidence of his terrible performance. In fact, the captain went to each of his teammates later and personally apologized for his effort.

"He made a contract with us that it

would never happen again. Ever," Riley said later. "That game was a blessing in disguise. It strengthened the fiber of this team. Ever since then, Kareem had this look, this air about him."

As the second game approached, the Lakers knew exactly what they had to do. "Our break starts with good tough defense," Rambis said. "That forces teams out of their offense. Then we must control the boards. That's where the work comes in. If we do those two things, the fast break is the easiest part."

Before Game Two on Thursday, Kareem went to Riley and asked if his father, Al Alcindor, could ride on the team bus to the Garden. Riley consented and then thought of his own father, Lee, who had been a minor league baseball manager. Just before he died, the elder Riley had told his son that someday he would have to make a stand, that someday he would have to kick some butt. Riley recalled those words to his players in his pre-game talk.

It was time, he said, to make a stand.

And they did. Kareem, in particular, reasserted himself with 30 points, 17 rebounds, eight assists and three blocks. Coop hit eight of nine from the floor to finish with 22 points. And like that, the Lakers evened the series, 109-102. Best of all, they had stolen a game in the Garden and now returned to the Forum for three straight.

"They expected us to crawl into a hole," Lakers assistant Dave Wohl said of the Celtics. "It's like the bully on the block who keeps taking your lunch money every day. Finally you get tired of it and you whack him."

They hosted the Celtics on Sunday afternoon and really whacked 'em again, returning the favor of Game One, 136-111. This time Worthy was the man, with 29 points. But Kareem's presence was felt again, too. He had 26 points and 14 rebounds.

At one point, Boston had led, 48-38, but Worthy dominated the second quarter and led Los Angeles to a 65-59 edge at intermission. The Lakers

The UCLA alums, Kareem and Bill, battled briefly in '87. (Bernstein photo)

Thompson gave the Lakers that frontcourt boost in '87. (Butler photo)

advantage, 107-105.

Boston always seemed to win the one- and two-point games, Coop said afterward. "Those are the games where you see the heart of a good ball team. We've just gotta buckle down and win one of these."

The opportunity was ripe with Game Five two nights later in the Forum. McHale answered the call for Boston, putting down 16 early points and forcing Riley to make a defensive switch in the second period. The L.A. coach put Kareem on McHale and left the shorter Rambis to contend with Parish. It worked immediately. The Lakers went on a 14-3 run at the close of the half to take a 64-51 lead. They stretched it to 89-72 after intermission, until the Celtics closed to within four at 101-97 with six minutes left. But Magic hit three shots and Kareem added four more, giving him 36 on the day, as the Lakers walked away with a 3-2 lead, 120-111.

"People didn't think we could win close games," Magic said afterward.

From there it went back to Boston. As usual, Jerry West didn't dare make the trip for fear of spooking the proceedings. Across the country old Lakers held their breath and watched the tube. After eight painful losses, this seemed to be the best chance yet to end Boston's domination. The Celtics would have to win the final two games. With a mere 38 hours rest between games, that just didn't seem possible for the boys from Beantown. And it wasn't. Kareem was there again, this time with 29 points, 18 of them in the second half when it mattered. The score was tied at 55 at intermission. Kareem had sat much of the second period in foul trouble while Kupchak did admirable work at backup.

The Celtics had played only seven people in the first half, and Magic could see that they were tired. It was written on their faces. Riley told him to keep pushing it at them, not to worry about turnovers. Just keep up the pressure. Keep pushing.

He did.

And the Celtics did something they had never ever done before. They

ran away in the second half, during which Kareem became the league's all-time leading playoff scorer with 4,458 points.

Bird, meanwhile, had fallen into a two-game shooting slump, going 17 for 42. He had been troubled by a chronically sore right elbow and bad back, although some speculated his real trouble was Coop's defense. Bird confirmed as much by refusing to offer excuses.

As with '84, the series was marked by physical play, although this time around it seemed to be the Lakers who were determined to gain an intimidation edge. "We're not out to physically harm them," Kareem

offered. "But I wouldn't mind hurting their feelings." Before Game Four, the NBA's vice president of operations, Scotty Stirling, warned each coach that fighting and extra rough play would be met with fines and suspensions. Riley told his players of Stirling's warning, but K.C. Jones chose not to. With their uninhibited play, the Celtics gained an edge, and the close game came down to one final Celtic possession. Bird had the ball but faced a double-team, so he dumped it off to Dennis Johnson above the foul line. From there, he drilled the winner with two seconds left. Boston had evened the series and regained its homecourt

A Showtime conference.

Coop and Bird.

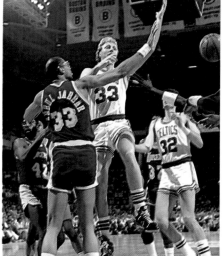

The Cap caps Bird.

Lord Byron.

Celebration '87. (Bernstein photos)

gave up a championship on their home floor, on the hallowed parquet, 111-100. McHale had kept them alive with 36 points, but he got his sixth foul with more than five minutes left. And, thanks in part to Coop's defense, Bird was closing out a 12-for-29 afternoon. "I thought I'd have a great game today," he said afterward.

In the end, the Lakers' victory was signalled by the squeaking of sneakers in the deathly quiet Garden as the crowd slipped away. It was the same crowd that had so riotously jostled the Lakers the year before.

"We made 'em lose it," Magic said

Kareem's retirement was inevitable, and Riley wanted to begin shifting the burden to other players.

with satisfaction.

Kareem was named the MVP. "He defies logic," Riley said of the 38-year-old Laker center. "He's the most unique and durable athlete of our time, the best you'll ever see. You better enjoy him while he's here."

Magic's trophy was sweet redemption, although he had said earlier that he didn't need any. "You wait so long to get back," he admitted afterward. "A whole year. That's the hard part. But that's what makes this game interesting. It's made me stronger. You have to deal with the different situations and see if you can come back."

Magic, certainly, had dealt. And there wasn't anybody watching pro basketball in 1985 who didn't believe that he would deal and deal again.

But before that could happen, the Lakers suffered yet another jolt. They ran through the 1985-86 season at their usual pace, only to lose to Houston 4-1 in the playoffs when the Rockets' Ralph Sampson hit a last-second shot in Game Five. Boston then whipped the Rockets for the '86 title, which brought the scorecard

Magic scores over D.J. in Game Six 1987. (Bernstein photo)

even. Magic's Lakers and Bird's Celtics had three championships apiece. In sports bars, living rooms and cocktail lounges across America, their competition spawned a running debate as to who was the greatest. Bird was named the league MVP for three consecutive seasons, 1984-86. On the heels of that, Red Auerbach went so far as to declare him the greatest basketball player ever.

Yet even as Bird claimed his awards, plenty of observers, including Chamberlain, thought Johnson was being shortchanged. "I don't know if there's ever been a better player than Magic," Wilt said.

Bird himself readily agreed. "He's the perfect player," he said of Magic.

GETTING BACK

With the disappointment of the '86 playoffs, West again reshuffled the lineup. McAdoo and Wilkes had left after the '85 season, and the Lakers had picked up veteran power forward Maurice Lucas in a trade, but he moved on before the '86-87 season opened. The future in the frontcourt became second-year forward A.C. Green, West's surprise steal of the 1985 draft.

Over the summer of 1986, Pat

Worthy began taking more of the offensive load in '87.

Thompson and Scott stepped up in '87. (Bernstein photo)

Laker parade.

Riley heard the question often. What did he think of Ralph Sampson's shot that killed the Lakers in the playoffs? Pretty soon, Riley fashioned a standard reply.

It was stimulation, he told his questioners. Stimulation for change.

Kareem was 40 years old heading into the 1986-87 season. As long as anyone could remember, he had been the focus of the Lakers' offense. But Riley wanted to change that. Kareem's retirement was inevitable, and Riley wanted to begin shifting the burden to other players. He wanted Magic, and to a lesser degree Worthy, to become the focus of the offense. So Riley and his staff began roughing up their ideas of how this transition should work. They took their notions into training camp that fall and were promptly confronted with confusion and frustration.

Riley then had second thoughts and told long-time Laker assistant Bill Bertka that maybe they should junk the idea.

No, Bertka replied, now is the time to make the change.

Within days, the players found their comfort zone in the new system. Kareem personally reassured Riley that everything was working fine. Then Magic sealed it in gold by turning in a stellar season, one that would make him the first guard since Oscar Robertson to win the league MVP award. His scoring zoomed to a career-high 23.9 points per game,

Bubbly time. (Bernstein photos)

and he was tops in the league in assists, at 12.2 per game.

He didn't do it alone, of course. Kareem. Worthy. Byron Scott. Cooper. A.C. Green. All of them wanted to establish their superiority. They constituted one of the greatest teams in basketball history, yet they were about to get even better.

The big boost arrived February 13, when the front office acquired Mychal Thompson from San Antonio. Bird was heartsick at the news. How could the

Spurs give Thompson to the Lakers? he asked. The 6'10" Thompson gave the Lakers just what they needed up front. He could play backup to Kareem at center, and he was a solid power forward. Better yet, he was an excellent low-post defender, and having played with McHale at the University of Minnesota, he knew better than anyone how to defend against Boston's long-armed forward. With Thompson, the Lakers surged to a 65-win regular season, the best in the NBA.

The Lakers were scorching. Detroit assistant Dick Versace scouted them during the playoffs and came away shaking his head. "They're cosmic," he said. "They're playing better than any team I've ever seen."

Denver fell 3-0 in the first round. Then Golden State dropped out of sight, 4-1. Seattle, the opponent in the Western Finals, could only have hoped to do as well. The Sonics went down, 4-0. Then the Lakers watched the Celtics eliminate Detroit in a seven-game Eastern Finals series.

Three days later, on Tuesday June 2, the Finals opened in the Forum before a crowd peppered with celebrity. The regulars, Jack Nicholson and Dyan Cannon, were there, but the series would attract oh so many more. Bruce Willis and Don Johnson. Whoopi Goldberg and John McEnroe. Johnny Carson and Henry Winkler. There were countless others. The media cited their presence as further proof that the Lakers offered more glitter than substance. This perception inflamed Riley. He had begun stewing with the end of the Eastern Finals, when the press described the injured Celtics as a blood-and-guts brigade. Riley threw this up to his troops as an affront. The Celtics get all the respect for being hard working, while the Lakers are packaged as a bunch of glitzy, super-talented guys who glide through their Showtime without much character or thought, Riley told his players. He considered the presence of all the celebs just another reason for the press to underestimate his team. "A bunch of glitter-group, superficial laid-backs," Riley spat. "This is the hardest-working team I've ever had, but regardless of what we do, we're minimized. . . We're empty people. . . and most of us aren't even from California."

The tirade brought puzzled looks from reporters, but most of them figured he was looking for something to whip his team to the next level. The long layoff had left some questions in his mind about intensity.

Riley was faced with two probable scenarios. Either the Celtics would come in game-sharp and take it to the

Worthy wanted the ball. (Bernstein photo)

Lakers, or they would come in weary from two straight seven-game battles. The latter very quickly established itself as the operating format for the day. Their tongues wagging, the Celtics could do little more than watch the Lakers run weave drills up and down the floor in Game One. "The Celtics looked like to me like they were keeping up pretty good," Mychal Thompson quipped, "just at a different pace."

Earvin led the rout with 29 points, 13 assists, 8 rebounds, and zero turnovers. On the receiving end of many of Johnson's passes, Worthy had 33 points and nine rebounds. The Lakers ran 35 fast breaks in the first two quarters and led by 21 at intermission. They settled into a canter thereafter, finally ending it, 126-113.

The Celtics knew they were reeling, and to catch themselves they had to stop Magic. Which they did in Game Two, but in the process they allowed Coop to switch specialties, from defense to offense. K.C. Jones put Danny Ainge on Magic and irritated him out of his brilliance. Boston trailed by seven in the second quarter, when Cooper pushed the Lakers through a 20-10 outburst, accounting for all 20 points himself by either scoring them or assisting. When it was over, he had laced in six of seven three-point attempts. And the Celtics had spent another day gasping in pursuit of the Laker break.

"One of the Laker girls could've scored a layup on us," Boston backup center Greg Kite said later.

Actually, the Lakers did quite well without the help of any of their girls. Kareem flicked in 10 of 14 shots for 23 points, while Magic put up nice boxy numbers, 20 assists and 22 points. In Coop's big second quarter, he racked up eight assists, tying a finals-series record. Cooper's six treys broke a playoff record, as well.

It all added up to a 141-122 rout, Boston's sixth straight road loss in the playoffs. Which left them eager to get back home. Bird, though, said he had his doubts about teammates who only played well in front of their families. Maybe, he said, it was time to get people who would play hard every night.

The L.A. papers enjoyed these developments thoroughly and took to calling the Celtics "Gang Green." Boston, however, answered rather nicely back in the Garden for Game Three. The Celtics big effort came in the second quarter when they hit 17 of 21 from the field (81 percent). The Lakers couldn't quite recover as Boston won, 109-103.

"I hope that's as well as they can play," Kareem said later.

For a brief moment the pressure was off the Celtics. No longer did they have to worry about the big embarrassment.

"We're just too good a team to be swept," Bird said. "This was the most important game of the series for us. If we lost, it might've been tough to get up for Game Four. Now it's going to be easy."

He was right. For more than three

quarters, Game Four would be easy. And the pressure would shift to the Lakers, which made Riley's mood even blacker. During a closed Los Angeles practice in the Garden, Riley requested that the cleaning staff leave the building. "Maybe he thought they had VCRs in their brooms," the Garden security director quipped. When they weren't playing cloak-and-dagger games, the Lakers were sequestered in their hotel rooms,

"Magic is a great, great basketball player," Bird said, settling the issue. "The best I've ever seen."

waiting on nightmarishly slow room service and jumping at the fire alarms that always greeted their stays in Boston. Any sane observer could have determined that the Lakers were too tight. But there weren't many sane observers around. This was the Lakers and the Celtics. And this was the Finals. Riley expected the worst.

He sure got it. Boston went up by 16 just after the half. Jack Nicholson, who had wormed a seat in the upper press area, spent most of the evening getting choke signs from Boston fans. "There was one guy," Nicholson said. "He was giving me the choke sign so

hard, I almost sent for the paramedics. He was wearing a gray sweat shirt, and his face turned almost as gray as his shirt. I couldn't believe it."

Shortly thereafter, relief came to Nicholson and the Lakers. L.A. cut the lead to eight with three and a half minutes to go in the game.

From there, the conclusion, the series actually, came down to one Magic sequence.

With half a minute left, the Lakers called time to set up a pick for Kareem. But Magic told Kareem to fake it as his defender, Parish, attempted to fight through the pick. When Parish tried to fight through, Kareem should roll to the basket, Magic said.

He did. The pass was there, and the Lakers took a 104-103 lead. But Bird grabbed it back at the 0:12 mark with a three-pointer, putting Boston up 106-104.

On the next possession, Kareem was fouled and went to the line, where he made the first and missed the second. McHale grabbed for the rebound, but the ball went out of bounds. McHale signalled Boston ball and had the boys in green headed back to the other end until the officials got their attention and notified them that it was Laker ball.

What followed of course was another of those plays for the ages. For years afterward, Magic would sit in the private screening room at his mansion, playing and replaying the scene thousands of times, each time tingling with a glee that would refuel his competitive fires. The play replenished his spirit every time he watched it.

Perhaps the definition of a Celtic hell is being assigned to Magic's screening room for eternity, watching the sequence and listening to his delighted laughter over and over and over.

Magic took the ball on the inbounds pass at the left of the key and at first contemplated a 20-footer, but McHale came out to change his mind. So Magic motored into the key, where Bird and Parish joined McHale in a trio of extended arms as Magic

Byron, A.C. and Coop matched the Pistons' bench in '88. (Bernstein photo)

lofted a hook. Parish almost brushed it. But the ball rose up and then descended to a swish. K.C. Jones, watching in a standing twist from the Celtic bench just feet away, felt his heart sink into an abyss.

The Celtics got a timeout with two seconds left, and the Lakers even left Bird open for a shot, which even went partially in. But it didn't stay down, and Magic ran off happily, having stolen Game Four, 107-106.

Red Auerbach, however, was anything but happy. He chased veteran official Earl Strom off the floor, and in front of the press contingency and the television cameras, he made pointed, disparaging remarks, suggesting that Strom was a gelding, that Strom had given the game to the Lakers.

Strom ducked into the officials dressing room, then stuck his head back out to tell Auerbach, "Arnold, you're showing the class that you always have."

Auerbach later explained that he chased Strom in an attempt to fire up his team. "People say, 'Relax, the game is over. The game is over.' Well, the game is never over," he said.

Alas, Red was wrong. The game was most definitely over, and Magic had retired to the locker room to be lost in his eternal joy. He dubbed the shot "my junior, junior, junior sky hook."

"You expect to lose on a sky hook," Bird said with a sickly smile. "You don't expect it to be Magic."

Would the game be remembered just for its last minutes? Bird was asked. "It should," he replied. "A lot happened in the last minute-and-a-half. Robert gets the ball taken away from him. I throw the ball at Kevin's feet. They miss a free throw, and we don't get the rebound. How many chances do you need to win a game?"

Then someone asked how he liked the Celtics' chances for the rest of the series. "How do I like my chances?" he asked and grinned. "How would you like it? I know, when we're up 3-1, I always say it's over. It's not a good position. There's no question

Showtime opens the '88 Finals.

Riley wanted the repeat. (Bernstein photos)

57

Magic hooks over Joe. (Kirthmon Dozier photo)

we're in trouble. We're not a good road team. I don't know if we can beat them twice out there. But we'll give it a try."

First, though, they had to win Game Five in the Garden. Magic almost closed out the series single handedly with 29 points, 12 assists, eight rebounds and four steals, but there wasn't much help. Before the game, Bird had told his teammates, "If they want to celebrate, let's not let them do it on the parquet." The Celtics had incentive enough, it seems. They got their second win, 123-108, and the series jetted back across the continent.

Kareem arrived for Game Six with a shave job on his balding head. And for a time, it seemed Los Angeles was intent on cutting it close. Magic had only four points by the half, and the Celtics led, 56-51. But like Kareem's pate, the Lakers glistened after intermission. Worthy finished with 22, and Kareem had 32 points, six rebounds and four blocks. Mychal Thompson had 15 points and nine rebounds. And Magic led them with another performance of all-around brilliance. On top of his previous efforts, his 16-point, 19-assist, eight-rebound showing brought him the MVP award. And Los Angeles claimed their fourth title of the decade, 106-93.

"Magic is a great, great basketball player," Bird said, settling the issue. "The best I've ever seen."

"He's the best in the game," Riley agreed. "He proved it in the regular season and the playoffs. We wouldn't be anywhere without him. We wouldn't be a championship contender without him."

Magic saw the reflection of his special talents in the team. "This is a super team, the best team I've played on," he said. "It's fast, they can shoot, rebound, we've got inside people, everything. I've never played on a team that had everything before. We've always had to play around something, but this team has it all."

Bird had to agree. "I guess this is the best team I've ever played against," he said. "In '85, they were good. In '84, I really thought they

Thompson dunks over Salley. (Butler photo)

The Lakers fought back in Detroit. (Bernstein photo)

should have beaten us. . . I don't know if this team's better than they were, but I guess they are. Their fast break is better. They're deeper."

The Lakers and Celtics had established a standard for pro basketball, and by 1987 they had begun to assume that the championship round was theirs to share. But there was a newcomer on the block, one quite eager to usurp their greatness. Before long, both teams would realize that Isiah Thomas and the Detroit Pistons were up to the challenge.

DO IT AGAIN?

To repeat.

That was Pat Riley's obsession.

Long before the Lakers had put the wraps on their 1987 title, he had begun plotting the course for the next season. Even as the champagne sprayed across the locker room in celebration, he was thinking about his first move. It would begin with a reporter's question. Riley waited until someone got around to asking if this Laker team could repeat as champions.

"I guarantee it," he said flatly.

The Lakers themselves were as surprised by this response as the reporters. But Riley was firm. He guaranteed it. That didn't exactly sit well with some of the players. The game was tough enough without asking for trouble and heaping on extra pressure. But Riley had done it.

Nineteen seasons had passed since the Celtics had won consecutive championships in 1968 and '69. Many observers had come to the conclusion that the feat couldn't be accomplished in the modern NBA. Riley rejected that notion. He believed that winning and winning again was a test of will, that greatness was available to the team that had the mental toughness to fight for it. He knew that the Lakers were a team of mentally strong individuals. They just needed someone to drive them to greatness. It was his job to do.

Beginning with training camp the next fall and throughout the following

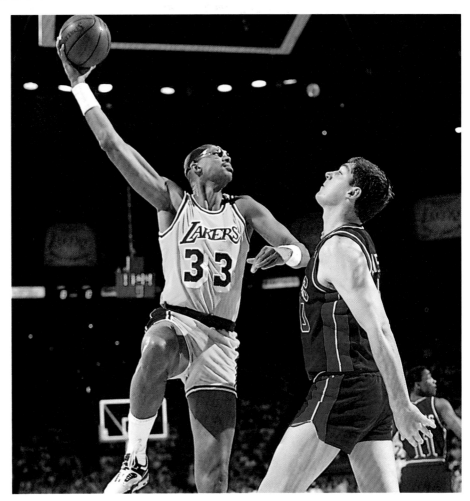

The sky hook was still a factor.

The Pistons surprised the Lakers in Game One. (Bernstein photos)

61

A.C. gets a defensive board in Game Four '89. (Butler photo)

approach to the game, not his physical talents, that set Isiah Thomas apart.

The other Pistons really desired to be NBA champions, but Thomas seemed entranced by the notion. He had spent his NBA career studying the people who won world championships, particularly his friend, Magic. Thomas wanted to know what they knew. For whatever reasons, he had turned this study into a mystical quest. He revered winners. Bird. Magic. Pat Riley. K.C. Jones. He wanted to be like them. He flattered them. Cajoled them. He wanted to duplicate their success. Whatever he could steal, he stole. The mannerisms were the easy part. Getting inside their minds was the real challenge. He wanted to think like an NBA champion.

He would pick Magic's brain in late-night phone calls to the West Coast. They would spend hours talking about what it took to win a championship. "I hate that I taught him," Magic would say later. "That's the only thing. I should go back and kick myself."

BACK TO BACK

It is important to note that he liked to be called James Worthy. Not Jim Worthy. Or Air Worthy. Or even Wings Worthy. Just James. In every facet of his life and his game, he seemed to opt for quiet dignity and grace rather than for flash and fame. It wasn't that he disliked the Hollywood aspect of playing for the Los Angeles Lakers. He just didn't immerse himself in it. Rather than own a mansion, he lived quietly with his wife Angela in a middle-class neighborhood in Westchester, not too far from the Forum. If he wanted, he could ride his bike to work. Other folks could take the limos.

Even so, he was the Lamborghini in the Laker fleet. At 6'9", James Worthy was incredibly quick and swift. No man his size in the league could stay with him. Without a doubt, Magic was the guard who drove the Showtime machine, but Worthy was the forward who made it go.

season, he pushed them like a man obsessed. He was Captain Ahab, and the back-to-back championship was the elusive great whale. On occasion the crew came close to mutiny, but then he would read their mood and lighten up just enough to keep them going.

The biggest factor, of course, was the team itself. They had the image of Showtime, of Magic's smile and the electraglide fast break, of run and gun and fun. But all in all they were a serious lot. Kareem and Worthy and A.C. Green were as businesslike as they come. Magic, too, had his fun face, but he had hardly been frivolous in his pursuit of basketball excellence over his career. As a team, they practiced like accountants. Detail mattered. Distraction wasn't tolerated. They had to be tough. They had to work. And they didn't slip often, but when they did, Riley was there to remind them, to irritate them with his

professorial tone and his mind games. In retrospect, Riley possibly burned out his relationships with his players during the 1987-88 season, which led to his leaving the Lakers after the 1990 playoffs.

In the end, the Lakers' intensity became a way of life. And quite simply, the Boston Celtics couldn't match it.

But there was a team in the Eastern Conference that could. The Detroit Pistons were driven by obsessions of their own. They, too, were a collection of mentally strong individuals, who like the Lakers, were led by a point guard with a beaming smile. But where Magic Johnson was 6'9", the Pistons' Isiah Lord Thomas II was a mere 6'1", a little man capable of dominating a big man's game. He was quick. He could leap. He could handle the ball like a showman. And he had taught himself to shoot. But it was his mental

Scott led the charge for Three-peat. (Gossage photo)

"Earvin can push the ball upcourt at an incredible tempo," Riley once explained. "But he needs someone even faster than himself to break for the wing and fly upcourt. James is the fastest man of his size in the NBA. In terms of finishing the fast break creatively and swiftly and deceptively, no one else compares."

And when the game slowed down a bit, Magic particularly enjoyed getting the ball to Worthy in the low post. Then, Magic said with a smile, it would be over in a matter of seconds.

"His first step is awesome," said former NBA forward Maurice Lucas.

As a veteran pro, Worthy showed an array of moves, a repertoire of head fakes and twitches and shifts that he used to reduce his defenders to nervous wrecks. "He'll give a guy two or three fakes, step through, then throw up the turnaround," Riley said. "It's not planned. It's all just happening."

Worthy had begun compiling this arsenal as a youngster in Gastonia, North Carolina. He would go to nearby Charlotte or Greensboro to catch occasional Carolina Cougar games in the ABA. His favorite was Doctor J., but Worthy studied them all. He was especially good at picking up their moves, then emulating what he had seen, practicing the steps and fakes over and over again before a mirror at home. He grew and became good enough with the moves to attract scholarship offers from colleges across the country. He flirted with the idea of joining Magic at Michigan State, but his heart was true Carolina blue. He opted to play at Chapel Hill for Dean Smith. Some observers have pointed out that Smith's controlled system kept Worthy's offensive potential tightly leashed, but James had no complaints. Smith turned the force loose just enough to allow Worthy to

lead the Tar Heels to the 1982 NCAA championship. He was named the tournament's Most Outstanding Player, and from there the pages just kept turning on the storybook.

He entered the draft as a junior that summer, and the Lakers snatched him up with the top pick. To the pro game, Worthy brought the same strong sense of security that had served him well at Carolina. He was coachable and patient and eager to learn. His physical skills and serious approach to the game made him an immediate fit in Los Angeles. He soon established a reputation for upping his level of play in the big games. Over his first five years in the league, he came to be known for his quiet excellence.

"I've always been the type of person who just wanted to play my own game," he explained.

As perfect as the story ran, the plot wasn't without its complications. In January of his freshman year at Carolina, he had shattered his ankle on a drive to the basket, and the injury required several operations and a determined rehabilitation. Then a similar injury sidetracked him as a rookie when he broke his leg just before the 1983 playoffs. He returned with a strong season in 1984 only to throw the bad pass in Game Two of the Finals that allowed the Celtics to avert disaster. But the worst turn came against Houston in the 1986 playoffs when his sub-par performance left Jerry Buss pondering a trade that would have sent Worthy to Dallas for Mark Aguirre and Roy Tarpley.

Jerry West interceded. Worthy was simply too good to trade, West thought. The Lakers' 1987 championship season only confirmed those beliefs. As time passed, it became more apparent that the Lakers would need Worthy's low-post game if Pat Riley's obsession with repeating was to be realized. With the 1987-88 season, Kareem would be 41, and while he was still the presence that the Lakers needed in their halfcourt game, he simply couldn't carry the load that he once had. Much of that burden would fall on the shoulders of James Ager Worthy.

Other people stepped forward to do their parts as well. Byron Scott began to realize his potential at shooting guard. He hadn't played well during the 1987 Finals, but the 1987-88 season brought new confidence. He led Los Angeles in scoring, averaging 21.7 points over the regular season while shooting .527 from the field. Also vital was the development of A.C. Green at power forward. He didn't shoot much but when he did the selection was pretty good. He rebounded well and continued to learn the intricacies of low-post defense.

Magic once again showed consistently brilliant play, although he missed 10 games at mid-season due to a groin injury. If there was a problem for the Lakers, it was Kareem's age. His decline was marked throughout the season, yet Mychal Thompson's presence off the bench provided just enough patchwork to make the Lakers effective in the post.

They even started the schedule with an 8-0 run, the finest opening in their history, and despite a series of ups and downs, they claimed the league's best regular-season record at 62-20. "Guaranteeing a championship was the best thing Pat ever did," Byron Scott said as the schedule drew to a close. "It set the stage in our mind. Work harder, be better. That's the only way we could repeat. We came into camp with the idea we were going to win it again, and that's the idea we have now."

Their path in the playoffs, however, quickly mired. They whipped San Antonio easily enough in the first round, but then they had to fight Utah through a seven-game death match. After that, Dallas was ready, and the Mavericks pushed the Lakers through another seven-game bout for the Western championship.

Then came Isiah Thomas's Pistons, who had defeated the Celtics to earn a trip to the Finals. Coached by Chuck Daly, the Pistons had acquired the nickname "Bad Boys" because of their tendency to give

Magic shone in '88. (Bernstein photo)

hard fouls and play physical defense. Their starting front line consisted of Bill Laimbeer, Rick Mahorn and Adrian Dantley. Joe Dumars ran the backcourt with Thomas. Beyond them, the Detroit bench was deep with veteran guard Vinnie Johnson and young forwards John Salley and Dennis Rodman.

As the series opened at the Forum on June 7, Magic made known his determination to win consecutive titles. Isiah allowed that he, too, was determined. Yet all this profession of determination was tempered a bit by the sight of Magic and Isiah holding hands and kissing before the Game

One tipoff. It was a display of brotherly love, they explained. That didn't stop it from wearing a bit thin as the series intensified.

Detroit wasted little time casting doubt on L.A.'s repeat plans. Dantley stepped forward in the first game, making 14 of 16 shots from the floor. Despite his best defensive efforts, A. C. Green watched helplessly as Dantley worked his peculiar offense. "It's so slow, you almost fall asleep," Green said of Dantley's shot. "He's got a slow release on it. You don't expect him to shoot it because of the timing, he's out of rhythm. You expect him to pass. And he has it back far

Green scores over Aguirre. (Butler photo)

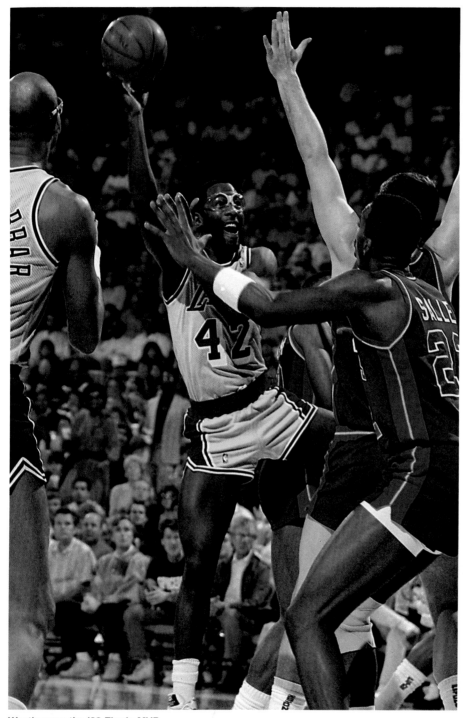

Worthy was the '88 Finals MVP.

Showtime. (Lipofsky photo)

enough, it's difficult to reach. He's developed that shot over his career."

Dantley's confidence was enough to lead the Pistons to a shocking 105-93 win and a 1-0 lead in the series. Suddenly, the Los Angeles press noticed that the Lakers bore a remarkably striking resemblance to the Celtics: i.e., old and tired. Showtime had just finished two seven-game series. Observers began wondering if they had enough left to get the rings.

As the shock of the loss wore off, the Lakers felt nothing but humiliation. "It was an embarrassing loss for us," Riley told reporters the next day. "The players came in this morning a little angry, a little upset and I hope they get worse. We're going to have to bring an attitude different than the one they took into Game One."

Actually, things looked bad for the Lakers. They were tired and down 1-0. They faced a confident, eager opponent. Then to make things worse, Magic came down with the flu. He played anyway and scored 23 points in Game Two. Worthy scored 26 while Scott had 24, and the Lakers charged back and evened the series with a 108-96 win. "I don't think there's any doubt Earvin Johnson showed the heart of a champion," Riley said afterward. "He was weak. Very weak. But this is what I call a hope game—you hope you get through it—and we got through it."

Game Three took the Finals to the Pontiac Silverdome, the football arena where crowds of 40,000 or more were

expected. On Sunday June 12, the Lakers regained the homecourt advantage with a 99-86 win. The main damage was done in the third period when Los Angeles shot 64 percent and outscored Detroit 31-14 to break open a one-point game.

Once again, Magic had shone despite his flu, with 18 points, 14 assists and six rebounds. The Lakers also got a solid inside game from A.C. Green, who had eight rebounds and scored 21 points by hitting nine of 11 from the field. Beyond that, he snuffed Dantley. The Pistons' forward had only 14 points, and scored just two in the second half.

Detroit came right back to take

It was hug time for the Lakers. Magic came out to meet Kareem. The crowd's applause was both large and warm.

Game Four, 111-86, as the love affair between Isiah and Magic turned into a scrap. Daly had been concerned that Johnson's smiling demeanor was stripping his players of some of their intensity. Those worries departed as

the Pistons focused their efforts on shutting down the Laker point guard. The main assignment went to Rodman. His annoying defense wore Johnson down and erased his perpetual smile.

"Magic is tough because he likes to penetrate," Rodman said afterward. "But I try to distract him, and hopefully he won't be able to look up the court and make one of those great passes."

Of the added defensive attention, Magic would only say, "[Rodman] doesn't frustrate me. I don't get frustrated. He creates some problems for me, but not a lot."

Yet anyone who witnessed the

runaway fourth quarter had to wonder. Magic certainly seemed frustrated. At one point, he knocked Isiah to the floor with an elbow, and Thomas leaped back up in his face. Afterward, the writers wanted to know if the friendship was off. "It was nothing personal—just business," Thomas replied.

"That's all it is," Magic agreed. "It's business."

Would it be forgotten? the writers asked.

"It's forgotten until Thursday," Magic said.

The Lakers opened Game Five with a fury of physical intimidation, scoring the game's first 12 points. But that approach soon stalled, then backfired.

"It seemed to me [the Lakers] were trying to be physical," Dantley said. "They made fouls they didn't have to make. It seemed they were trying to say, 'Hey, we can play physical.' Then they had all their big guys on the bench."

Dantley played a major role, scoring 25 points, 19 of them in the first half, to pace the Pistons to another win, 104-94. Once again, it was a total domination made possible because the Lakers had gotten away from what they did best—rebounding and running. "We couldn't contain anyone on the boards," Riley said. "We had [two] defensive boards in the fourth quarter and they had 10 offensive boards. You're not going to beat anyone with that."

Detroit held a 3-2 lead, and Pat Riley's dream seemed to have gone gray. But the Lakers were hardly shaken. The Pistons would have to claim the championship in the Forum, and that wouldn't be a cakewalk. The series came down to a classic confrontation, and both sides responded appropriately.

The Lakers took a 53-46 halftime lead in Game Six, then held on while Isiah went wild in the third period. Despite spraining his ankle, Thomas scored 25 points in the period, an NBA Finals record. Worthy and Magic answered for the Lakers and the game went down to the wire.

With a minute left, the Pistons held

a 102-99 edge. They were mere 60 seconds from an NBA title, the franchise's first ever. The league trophy was even wheeled into the Pistons' locker room. Iced champagne was brought in. CBS requested the presence of team owner Bill Davidson to receive the trophy. Minutes later, those plans were rapidly disassembled, the trophy taken away before Davidson could feel it.

"A minute is a long time," Magic would say later. "A long time. It's just two scores and two stops and you're ahead."

The first Laker score came on

At last, the league had a repeat champion. The Lakers had grasped the greatness about which Riley had rhapsodized so often.

Byron Scott's 14-foot jumper to bring L.A. within one, 102-101, at 52 seconds. Detroit struggled for the right shot on its possession and failed when Thomas missed an 18-footer. At 14 seconds, Kareem positioned for his skyhook from the baseline, and Laimbeer was whistled for a foul, which he and the Detroit bench protested profusely. Kareem made both free throws, giving L.A. a 103-102 lead.

Although they had lost their lead, the Pistons couldn't have asked for a better position. They had the ball and a chance to win it. At eight seconds, Dumars took the shot for Detroit, a six-foot, double-pumper. The ball seemed to hang in midair, then caught the rim and fell away. The rebound slipped through Dennis Rodman's frantic hands, and Scott controlled the loose ball. Like that, the Lakers had tied the series.

For Game Seven, L.A. got going behind Worthy's low-post scoring and raced to a seemingly insurmountable lead, 90-75, in the fourth quarter. Yet just when Riley could taste the reality of his repeat fantasy, the Lakers got fat. Seemingly headed down in a blowout, the Pistons found a way back. Daly went with a pressure lineup that consumed the Lakers' lead in gulps. At 3:52 Salley knocked in two free throws to close to 98-92, and the Lakers were in obvious panic. At 1:17, Dumars, who led the Pistons with 25 points, hit a jumper to make it 102-100. But Magic scored a free throw off a Rodman foul, stretching it to 103-100. Detroit then had its best opportunity, but Rodman took an ill-advised jumper at 39 seconds. Scott rebounded and was fouled. His two free throws pushed the lead to 105-100. After Dumars made a layup, Worthy hit a free throw and Laimbeer canned a trey, pushing the score to 106-105 with six seconds showing. Green completed the scoring with a layup, making it 108-105, and although the Pistons got the ball to Isiah at midcourt with a second remaining, he fell without getting off a shot.

Riley could only give thanks. "It was a nightmare to the very end," he said. "I kept saying, 'Please don't let this end in a nightmare.' We were a great team trying to hold on. Hey, they just put on one of the greatest comebacks in the history of this game and they have nothing to be ashamed of. We're a great team and they had us hanging on at the end. We were able to do it because of who we are, but they gave us all we could handle."

As frantic as the closing had been, the Lakers had done the impossible.

Not only had they repeated, they'd won three seven-game battles to get the title. Nobody could say they hadn't earned it.

Worthy had racked up 36 points, 16 rebounds and 10 assists, a monster triple double if there ever was one. For that and his earlier efforts in the series, he was named the MVP. Self-effacing as usual, Worthy said he would have voted for Magic. "Then," he added I'd have to vote for myself for the first time in my career."

At last, the league had a repeat champion. The Lakers had grasped the greatness about which Riley had rhapsodized so often. They were all relieved. And to make sure Riley had no more wise ideas about the future, Kareem kept his eye on the coach during the post-game interviews. It did little good, though. Riley already was working on a name for the next chapter of the Laker adventure.

He planned to call it "Three-peat," a phrase coined by Byron Scott.

For most of the 1988-89 season, the Lakers looked good to make it three straight. They finished the regular season at 57-25, and Riley had gone so far as to patent his Three-peat slogan in hopes of cashing in on the souvenir market. His prospects for big royalties seemed to improve with each round of the playoffs.

The Lakers swept their way along an 11-0 run to the Finals. Portland, Seattle and Phoenix—each went out with the dustpan. The wins meant that Riley needed only one more victory to become the winningest coach in playoff history. He might have gotten it but for a pair of hamstrings, one belonging to Byron, the other to Magic.

At the outset, the potential for drama seemed high. The Pistons were back in the Finals, eager to redeem themselves from the year before. And the 42-year-old Kareem had announced his retirement effective at the close of the season. The Lakers hoped to send him out with another ring. But the dramatic possibilities began to soften before Game One in Detroit, when Byron

Coop filled in when Magic and Byron went down. (Laker photo)

Scott suffered a severe hamstring injury. He would miss at least the first two games, the injury report said.

The Lakers missed him and more in Game One. With six minutes left, Detroit led, 97-79. After the late patty-cakes, they finished it, 109-97. As expected, the Lakers snapped right back in Game Two to take a 62-56 lead at intermission; Coop was hitting; and Magic had that look in his eye. But events turned upside down in the third. With about four minutes left, Salley blocked a Mychal Thompson shot, starting the Detroit fastbreak the other way. Magic dropped back to play defense, and in so doing, pulled his hamstring. He sensed immediately that the injury was serious and flailed at the air in frustration. He didn't return after that.

"I felt a twinge early in the third quarter but thought everything was okay," Johnson said later of the injury. "Then on that last play I pulled it trying to get back on defense."

Even without Magic, the Lakers battled furiously and almost pulled even at the end. But Isiah hit two free throws with a second remaining to give the Pistons a 2-0 lead, 108-105.

With the series shifting to the Forum, the speculation centered on Magic. Could he play?

He tried.

But he left Game Three in the first quarter with the Lakers leading 11-8. "I wanted to play so bad, but I just could not," Johnson said later. "I could not make the cuts, defensively, that I had to make."

"He made a heck of an effort,"

Dumars said, "but it just wasn't there. You could tell by his motion. One time, the ball was right there a couple feet away, and he just couldn't get it."

Without him, the Lakers still did a fair imitation of a championship contender. Worthy scored 26, and Kareem played out of his 42-year-old body, scoring 24 points with 13 rebounds. The only veteran in the backcourt, Coop had 13 assists and 15 points. Grand as it was, that didn't do it.

The Pistons slipped away with yet another game, 114-110.

Down 3-0, the Lakers still talked of making history. Specifically, they would have to be the first team to ever overcome a three-game deficit. Tony Campbell, who had filled in admirably at guard for Scott, asserted that such a comeback was in the works.

Wiser voices weren't quite so optimistic.

"It's like you have a real nice sports car and a great driver," Kareem said of the circumstances, "and then all of a sudden you have to find somebody who has been driving a bus to be a driver. That's a learning experience."

Going in, the Lakers knew things would be tough. Riley told Worthy that he would have to up his game a few notches and get them a win. Riley reminded Worthy how his efforts had paid off in '88. And Worthy responded with a championship effort—40 points on 17 of 26 from the floor, and that with Mahorn jawing in his face every other step of the way. But he couldn't do it alone.

The Forum crowd had come expecting an event, Kareem's final game. The big center had conducted his final warmup, his pate glistening a regal green and red from the Forum lights. He was composed, spending much of the session standing silently in a half slouch, his hand on his hip. The Cap did one final finger roll and headed down to the bench. With that signal, the team had followed, igniting a growing applause that spread across the Forum crowd.

Once the game started, the pattern was familiar. Mahorn and Coop mixed it up in the first period, drawing a double technical. With Worthy playing out of his mind, the Lakers took a 35-23 lead at the end of the first. But Detroit closed the gap to 55-49 at intermission. Then the Bad Boys jumped out in the third, starting with an opening trey by Laimbeer. Mahorn then scored four quick points, and the Pistons took a 59-58 lead moments later when Dumars hit a driving bank shot, drew the foul and made the free throw, giving him 19 points on the evening. Mahorn followed that with another bucket, and suddenly it was time-out L.A.

When Worthy blasted them back into the lead later in the quarter, the crowd got loud with a chant of "Three-peat." It was nice Hollywood stuff, but it would never see the light of reality. They nipped and tucked it a ways from there. The Lakers held a 78-76 lead at the end of the third, but everybody in the building sensed it was over. As the Pistons' momentum grew, the Lakers appeared drained.

When Detroit got the ball back with 3:23 left and leading 100-94, the crowd rose to a standing ovation, not to try and pull a miracle out of exhaustion, just a note of thanks. Kareem came back in the game, but neither side could get it right. The next two minutes was an exchange of missed shots and turnovers.

At 1:37, Kareem broke the chill with a spin move and bank shot, his last NBA points, bringing the Lakers to 100-96. But the Pistons surged away again to a 105-97 finish. As the time wound down, Riley sent Orlando Woolridge in for the Cap. It was hug time for the Lakers. Magic came out to meet Kareem. The crowd's applause was both large and warm, and the Pistons all joined in.

"Kareem. Kareem. Kareem," the crowd intoned over and over.

It was much more, however, than a spirited closing to a frustrating playoff. It was a celebration of a decade, perhaps the grandest 10 seasons in all of pro sports.

Red, of course, might argue about that. But just about everyone else would agree. These Lakers were the best ever.

The Lakers went to the Finals eight times in 10 years. (Bernstein photo)

Earvin. The ultimate big guard. (Gonzalez photo)

Mr. MVP

Earvin Johnson joined an elite club last May when he was voted the NBA's Most Valuable Player for the third time in four seasons. Kareem won the award six times during his 20-year NBA career. Bill Russell won it five, and Wilt Chamberlain four. Magic, Larry Bird and Moses Malone have claimed three each.

Observers have pointed out that Magic is the only guard to have won the award more than once. But perhaps that isn't a fair distinction, because Earvin is far more than just a guard for the Lakers. He rolls the positions of guard, forward and center into one player.

The award came just days after Los Angeles was eliminated by Phoenix in the 1990 playoffs.

"This makes my week better,"

Magic said. "It's a good feeling at an otherwise bad time."

The award also recognized the dramatic shift Johnson had made in his game to compensate for the loss of Kareem, who had retired after the 1989 season. He became responsible for more of the team's offense and upped his scoring to 22.3 points per game, with many of the extra points coming from a barrage of three-pointers.

"I had to do different things," Magic said. "My whole role changed and it was a challenge. The three-point shot gave my game much more versatility. I was harder to guard. And without Kareem, I wound up posting up more than I ever had. And I think I became good at that.

"With Kareem, you knew the ball would go inside to him first and we'd

Magic and Isiah are close friends. (Dozier photo)

73

Magic takes on former teammate Norm Nixon in a 1985 chess match. (Bernstein photos)

Who, me?

The power forward.

Gotcha.

feed off of that. I might get it back if the ball swung around, or if I wanted to go into a two-man game. But now, with me posting up on a regular basis and looking for the three-pointer, I wasn't only running the show and setting the table for everyone else. I was also actually involved as part of the offense. Suddenly, I had different responsibilities."

His new role was a major reason the Lakers rang up a league-best 63 wins last season. Magic averaged 11.5 assists per game and led the league in triple doubles with 11.

"He's the one player I'd pay to see play," said longtime rival Bird.

"He's at another plateau," agreed Phoenix Coach Cotton Fitzsimmons. "The MVP is a guy who leads his team and sacrifices for his team to win. [Magic] epitomizes that."

"Magic is the best player that's come down the pike in a long time,"

"In my days of playing basketball, I don't think I've ever seen a greater player or a greater winner."

—Jerry West

Portland's Buck Williams said after the award was announced.

Magic dedicated his 1987 MVP award to his father, Earvin, Sr. For 1989, he dedicated it to his mother, Christine, and himself. The latest award honors his fifth grade coach and teacher, Jim and Greta Dart.

"They helped me go to camps and got me started," he said of the Darts. "I appreciate everything they did for me. They're like my godparents."

The award only confirmed what Lakers General Manager Jerry West has been thinking for some time. "I'm not a person who likes to compare players," West said. "But in my days of playing basketball, I don't think I've ever seen a greater player or a greater winner in my life."

Magic works on Mike.

The perennial all star. (Bernstein photos)

In the early days he was a dunkmaster. (Laker photos)

Coop de Grace

He came into the league in 1978 as a high-flying unknown out of New Mexico State, a third-round pick with a slim chance of making the roster. But Michael Cooper stayed with the Lakers for 12 seasons and in the process endeared himself to a generation of Forum regulars.

His special tenure in Los Angeles ended over the summer when the 34-year-old Cooper asked to be placed on waivers so that he could accept a lucrative offer to play for an Italian team. The timing of his departure meant there was no opportunity for the fans to bid him farewell.

That probably wasn't necessary anyway, though. The crowd virtually celebrated his every move over the years. His appearance in each game would bring a chorus of "Coop, Coop," rolling down from the Forum rafters.

There is no better indication of his classiness than the evolution of his game. He was what they used to call "a leaper," able to execute a dunk with ease. His crowd-pleasing shot in the early days was his "Coop-a-Loop," the back-door slam that always worked to gas up the house. But Coop was never merely addicted to acrobatics. His love was the game itself. So while his legs were gradually losing their spring, he was adapting his game. He made the three-pointer his offensive weapon, and he used it to kill the spirits of Laker opponents at just the right moment in games.

His real identity, however, came from his defense, which he used to smother Boston's Larry Bird during the Celtics/Lakers bashes of the mid 1980s. Coop's special tenacity was acknowledged in 1987 when he was named the NBA Defensive Player of the Year. The Magic/Bird competition was indeed a major factor in the NBA's increasing popularity over the past decade, and Coop played an important role in those showdowns. His dedication to stopping Bird has become one of pro basketball's enduring legends, and today Coop has no greater admirer than Bird himself.

It should come as no surprise that Coop was also an iron man, at one point in his career appearing in 455 consecutive games. His consistency meant that his teammates could count on him night after night and seldom be disappointed.

The accompanying photos are meant as a salute to Coop. L.A. will always be his town, and the Forum his crowd.

Shooting the trey.

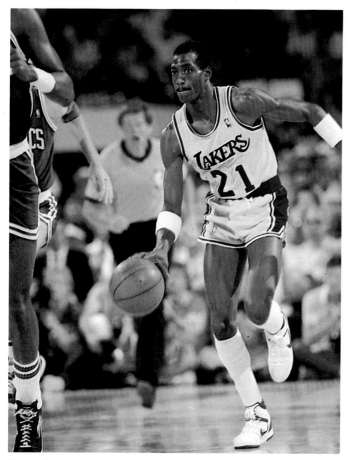

The style.

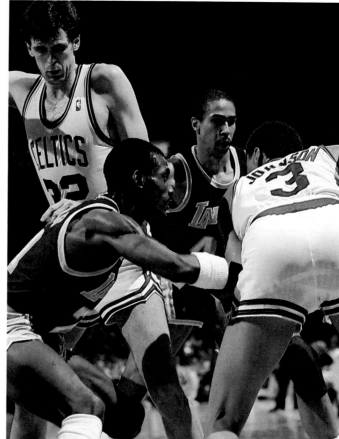

The tenacity.

He shut down Bird in '87. (Bernstein photos)

Trey time.

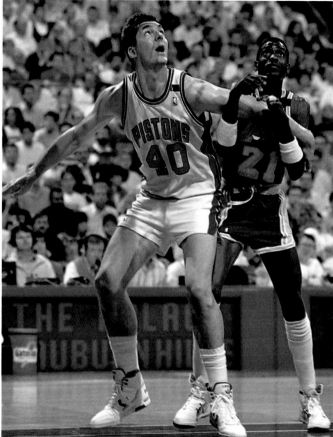

The battles.

Coop fights through a Mahorn pick in the '89 finals. (Bernstein photos)

West and his Lakers battled the Celtics six times in the Finals.

The Lone Thread

Y ou don't have to spend too much time with Jerry West, perhaps a matter of minutes, before you sense his anguish. It's not a flaming pain, but a deep, slow-burning one, a complicated anxiety, the kind that can kill people, especially former great athletes. But right now, it's not killing Jerry West. Instead he wears this anguish like an after shave.

He, as you probably know, is the celebrated general manager of the Los Angeles Lakers. Before that, he was one of the greatest basketball players ever. That should be enough for anybody, you would think. But it obviously isn't enough for Jerry West. Which makes you wonder why.

How can one person demand so much of life?

As an executive, Jerry West still travels like a player. A single road bag. His crisp white dress shirt neatly tucked inside with his other items. No hangers. No suit bag. He's still a spartan, still moves as unencumbered as he did when he ran the point for the Lakers for 14 seasons. He still glides through his tasks with a proficiency that startles the opposition.

The real baggage for Jerry West is the memories from his playing days. On one hand, he professes not to have any. On the other, he calls them up from the file in his head with startling clarity.

Six times in the 1960s, he and the Lakers faced the Boston Celtics in the National Basketball Association Finals. Six times they lost. On their seventh try for a championship, the Lakers met the New York Knicks. They lost again. They finally won in

In Jerry West's mind, there was no enemy. There was only the obstacle, and that was the game itself

1972, then lost an eighth time in the Finals the next year.

"I don't think people understand there's a real trauma associated with losing," he said in a recent interview. "I don't think they realize how miserable you can be. Particularly me. I was terrible. It got to the point with me that I wanted to quit basketball. I really did. I didn't think it was fair that you could give so much and play until there was nothing left in your body to give and you couldn't win. It really was frustrating."

Yet the more elusive it proved to be, the more the championship came to have an almost mesmerizing hold on him. "The closer you get to the magic circle, the more enticing it becomes," he said. "I imagine in

some ways, it's like a drug. It's seductive because it's always there, and the desire is always there to win one more game. I don't like to think I'm different, but I was obsessed with winning. And losing made it so much more difficult in the offseason."

He played college basketball at West Virginia, and as a 6'3" junior forward he led the Mountaineers to the 1959 NCAA championship game where they lost by a point. "I had my hands on the ball about midcourt with no time left on the clock," he recalled, "and I said, 'If I could have just gotten one more shot...' But it wasn't to be. Those are the things that stay with you more than the wins. Those are the things that really are wearing.

"My basketball career has sort of been on the tragic side of everything. It hasn't been on the positive side. It was so close, yet so far away."

It seems logical that at least part of his current anguish stems from those frustrations. But only West knows for sure. Or maybe nobody knows. But West does know this—no matter how great he was way back when, he has accomplished things now as general manager of the Lakers that he never accomplished as a player. Specifically, he has vanquished the Boston Celtics and the rest of the NBA. But that's a paradoxical knowledge for West. It both increases and lessens his anguish all at the same time.

It wasn't that the Celtics and Knicks were the enemy. In Jerry West's mind, there was no enemy. There was only the obstacle, and that was the game itself. His unfortunate compulsion was perfection in a game that never allows it.

Yet he has come as close as

anyone. One great night as a player, he made all 12 of his free throws and 16 of 17 field goal attempts. He also had 10 rebounds, 12 assists and 10 steals.

"I had nights when you just couldn't guard me," he said.

But the closer he seemed to get to perfection, the more his anxiety increased. The same could be said of him as a general manager.

In the 1980s, the Lakers won five NBA World Championships. But that is old hat now to Jerry West. The Lakers went 63-19, the best regular-season record in the league last season, but they lost in the second round of the playoffs. The Lakers have gone two straight years without a championship.

West is not a happy man these days. This team should be doing better, he tells himself. "The expectations are awfully high around here," he explains. The translation, of course, is that *his* expectations are awfully high. Always have been.

Watching Jerry West, you think if there really is a Field of Dreams, it should be for this guy. Somebody should be hearing the voice.

Ease his pain.

THE FIRST AND THE LAST

West says that he has consciously blocked out his memories of the Lakers' championship battles with the Celtics. The only recollections he keeps fresh are of the first title series with Boston in 1961 and the last in 1969.

The first was noteworthy, West says, because the Celtics had a much better team but the Lakers still had a chance to win it. The series went to a seventh game, and in the closing seconds at Boston Garden, Laker forward Frank Selvy took a shot from the baseline that would have given Los Angeles its first championship. Selvy was usually a deadeye, but his shot just missed, and while Elgin Baylor was underneath to put it back in for the Lakers, Boston's Sam Jones shoved him out of bounds and got the ball. The Celtics went on to win in

West at West Virginia. (WVU photo)

overtime. It was then, West says, that first he realized the Lakers did not have good fortune on their side.

That feeling would return to him again and again over the coming decade. Los Angeles lost to Boston again the next year. And in '65 when Baylor went down with a knee injury. And in '66 and '68.

Then came 1969. The Lakers had acquired Wilt Chamberlain and for the first time had a real center to battle Russell. The Celtics, meanwhile, had struggled through the regular season only to find new life in the playoffs. For the first time, Los Angeles had the homecourt advantage.

"Most of the years we played they were better than we were," West said of the Celtics. "But in '69 they were not better. Period. I don't care how many times we played it, they weren't better. We were better. Period. And we didn't win. And that was the toughest one."

Determined not to face another championship loss, West came out smoking. He scored 53 in the first game, while Chamberlain and Russell engaged in an old-men's struggle underneath. John Havlicek scored 39 for Boston, but the Lakers nudged an advantage and won, 120-118.

Afterward, West was so tired he iced down his arms. Russell called West's show "the greatest clutch performance ever against the Celtics."

"It wasn't his 53 points that beat us," Russell said. "It was his 10 assists."

The Lakers won again at home, then lost the first game in the Garden. But the Celtics were obviously winded. Game Four provided the real opportunity for the Lakers to strike the death blow. It was what some might call one of those old-fashioned furious defensive struggles that Russell loved to wage. Others would call it just plain ugly. The two teams combined for 50 turnovers and enough bad shots and passes to last them a month. After Game One, the Celtics had taken to double-teaming West, forcing him to make the pass rather than take the shot. That had slowed the Lakers' scoring, and it again worked in the fourth game. Over the final four minutes, the two teams had one basket between them. But with 15 seconds left, the Lakers had an 88-87 lead and the ball. All they had to do was get the pass in safely and run out the clock. Instead, Boston's Em Bryant stole it and the Celtics raced the other way. Sam Jones missed the jumper, but Boston controlled the rebound and called time at 0:07. On the inbounds, Bryant threw the ball to Havlicek, then set a pick to his left. Don Nelson and Bailey Howell followed in line to make it a triple pick. At the last instant, Havlicek passed to Sam Jones, cutting to his right. Jones stumbled to a halt behind Howell, who cut off West. There, at the 0:03 mark, Jones lofted an 18-footer. He slipped as he took the off-balance shot, and it just cleared Chamberlain's outstretched hand. Jones knew it was going to miss and even tried to pull it back, he explained afterward. The ball went up anyway, hit on the rim, rose up, hit the back of the rim and fell in. Chamberlain leaped up and lorded over the basket, his face a picture of anguish as the ball came through the net.

Boston had tied the series at two all, 89-88, and a dagger in West's heart wouldn't have felt any worse.

"It got to the point where I didn't think I was doing enough. I was searching everything that I had ever done in my life for a reason, looking for an answer why. Why couldn't we win it? "

West versus the Knicks in 1970.

"The Lord's will," he said later.

"I thought to shoot it with a high arc and plenty of backspin," Jones told the writers. "So if it didn't go in, Russell would have a chance for the rebound."

Russell wasn't even in the game, one scribe pointed out.

"What the hell," Boston's Larry Siegfried said. "You hit a shot like that, you're entitled to blow a little smoke about arc and backspin and things like that."

Once again the Celtic luck had prevailed, but the Lakers regrouped and headed home for Game Five. Back in the Forum, the Celtics just didn't have it. Russell scored two points with 13 rebounds. Chamberlain owned the inside, with 31 rebounds and 13 points, while West rained down from the perimeter with 39 points. Boston fell, 117-104, and trailed 3-2.

West, though, had badly injured his hamstring and was hobbled. He

played in Game Six and scored 26. But the Lakers needed more from him. And certainly more from Chamberlain, who made a measly two points. Boston won, 99-90, and tied the series at 3.

Once again a Celtics/Lakers series had come down to a seventh game. Only this time, Game Seven was in Los Angeles, this time there wouldn't be a Garden jinx. Or would there? West's hamstring had worsened. It was wrapped, and he declared himself ready to go. But everyone wondered. Everyone except Lakers owner Jack Kent Cooke.

As the series returned to California, Cooke began planning his victory celebration. He visualized the perfect finale for a championship season. He ordered thousands of balloons suspended in the Forum rafters. According to Cooke's plan, they would be released as the Lakers claimed their championship. As the balloons rained down on the jubilant

Lakers and their fans, the band would strike up "Happy Days Are Here Again." Cooke could see it clearly.

And so could Red Auerbach. The Celtics' general manager walked into the Forum that May 5 and gazed up into the cloud of balloons in the rafters. "Those things are going to stay up there a hell of a long time," he said.

No one was more infuriated by the balloons than Jerry West. The thought of them made him sick with anger. "That just wasn't my style," he said. The Celtics, always looking for that extra little boost of emotion, found it in the Forum rafters. They hit eight of their first 10 shots on the way to a big lead, but then had to hang on in the fourth quarter as West and the Lakers charged back (Chamberlain was on the bench with a leg injury). Boston had just enough left to claim yet another championship, 108-106.

West, of course, was disgusted with another loss. He had finished with 42 points, 13 rebounds and 12 assists. The Celtics went to the Los Angeles locker room immediately after the game. First Russell took West's hand and held it silently. Then Havlicek professed, "Jerry, I love you."

"He is the master," Siegfried said of West. "They can talk about the others, build them up, but he is the one. He is the only guard."

West was named the MVP, the first and only time in NBA Finals history that the award has gone to a member of a losing team. The gestures were nice, West said, but they didn't address his agony.

"I didn't think it was fair," he said in 1990, "that you could give so much and maybe play until there was nothing left in your body to give, and you couldn't win. It was like a slap in the face, like, 'We're not gonna let you win. We don't care how well you play.' I always thought it was personal.

"It got to the point where I didn't think I was doing enough. I was searching everything that I had ever done in my life for a reason, looking for an answer why. Why couldn't we win it? That's why it became so personal. It almost controlled my life."

Cooke, meanwhile, was left with the task of figuring out what to do with all the balloons. He finally decided to send them to a children's hospital.

The Lakers lost the next Finals to New York, then in 1971 they got shoved aside in the Western playoffs by Lew Alcindor and the Milwaukee Bucks. By 1972, time was running out for Los Angeles. Bill Russell had been out of basketball for two years, and the Lakers still didn't have a championship. Chamberlain had turned 35, and West was 33.

Cooke decided to try a new coach and hired 45-year-old Bill Sharman, the former Boston Celtic who had just coached the Utah Stars to the 1971 American Basketball Association championship. He led the Lakers to a remarkable 69-13 record and yet another shot at the championship. Once again, the Finals foe was the Knicks. Primed at last to win it, the Lakers stumbled and lost the first

game. But they gathered their composure and took the second in a show of power. Luck had always been such a big factor for the Lakers. Each of the previous Finals, they were overcome with a sense that fortune had turned against them. But that all changed after Game Two in 1972. That night West lay awake wondering how he would act if they actually had a championship to celebrate. He wasn't a drinker or a whoop-it-up type. How would he act?

Despite West's shooting slump, they went on to claim the next three games and their first championship. Chamberlain was the MVP. But for West, the finish was rife with irony.

"Every once in a while, when you get something done as a general manager, you really feel good abut it. You really do. Finding and drafting players and watching them develop, that's where you get your satisfaction."

—Jerry West

After years of losing, his emotions were nearly empty, and when the Lakers got it, the championship seemed anti-climactic. "I played terrible basketball in the Finals," he said in 1990. "And we won. And that didn't seem to be justice for me personally, because I had contributed so much in other years when we lost. And now, when we won, I was just another piece of the machinery. It was particularly frustrating because I was playing so poorly that the team overcame me.

"Maybe," he said after a moment's thought, "that's what the team is all about."

THE PLAYER, THE MANAGER

Today, Jerry West remains a piece

of the machinery, a very big piece. Fred Schaus, who coached him at West Virginia and later with the Lakers, says West has become the premier general manager of his time. What Red Auerbach did with the Celtics in the 1960s and '70s, West has done with the Lakers in the '80s and '90s, Schaus said. "I admired Auerbach in the past, and I admire West now. Their teams are finishing high in the standings and they're drafting low. That's why it's so hard to remain competitive."

West has said many times that his success as a general manager—"If I've had any," he says—has nothing to do with the competitiveness he showed as a player.

"I have to disagree with him," Schaus said. "Play golf with him, or any game of skill. Cards or anything. He's such a competitor. He wants to be the very best at doing anything."

Told of Schaus's comment, West acknowledged that competitiveness does drive him as a GM. "But it's so different," he said. "Being a player, it's a wonderful feeling to win an important ball game, to compete against the best players. Being a general manager is so much more subtle, so much more frustrating. It's a completely different feeling. Every once in a while, when you get something done as a general manager, you really feel good about it. You really do. Finding and drafting players and watching them develop, that's where you get your satisfaction."

But by and large, West gets far more agony than satisfaction from his job. During games he's a bundle of nervous energy and often winds up out in the Forum parking lot while the outcome is being settled. It's similar to the agony he felt as the Lakers coach in the late 1970s, when he felt frustrated that most of his players just couldn't do the things that he used to do on the court.

Such irritations are the lot of former greats who are left to get their basketball thrills vicariously. Today, West will occasionally pick up a ball and take a few shots. "Then I'll wonder, 'What the hell am I doing this for?'" he says. "It's a part of my life that was there at one time, and it's not there now."

Still, his experiences as a player are the foundation for his beliefs and prejudices as a GM.

Some examples:

1) He believes that young players with great potential must have playing time.

The Lakers drafted West, a skinny 6'3" forward in 1960, and also picked his college coach, Schaus, as the team's new head coach. That was good and bad, West says. Good that Schaus knew him as a person, but bad because Schaus wanted to bring him along slowly. For the first 20 games or so, West sat the bench and found the time as a spectator unbearable. He let Schaus know that he didn't like it. "I could not learn sitting on the bench," he said. "The only thing I could learn were bad habits. I had to get out there and get over those first year jitters." He knew he could compete on a higher level than the average player. But no matter how hard he tried, or how well he played in practice, his playing time seemed set. As badly as the team needed West's scoring, Schaus remained reluctant to place the burden on his rookie.

Finally, with the team's record sinking, Schaus gave West the nod. "All of a sudden things weren't very good," West said, "and I had a chance to step in and start, and I never gave it up."

The Lakers began a turnaround with West in the lineup, although it was nothing that he engineered by himself. Elgin Baylor was in his prime, playing the forward spot in spectacular fashion. With each passing game, it became more obvious they were something special. Baylor was the acrobatic wonder inside, and West gained confidence running the team.

At times, though, West tended to brood over the flaws in his game, Schaus said. "When he was not playing well, he'd kind of go into a shell. He wouldn't talk to anybody, not the coaches or his own teammates. If he wasn't playing well, he was tough

to live with."

"I was nervous all the time," West said. "But then again, I was a nervous player. That's where I got my energy from."

2) He is very sensitive about player personnel issues, particularly trades.

After he had been with the Lakers several years, West heard that Schaus wanted to trade him to the Knicks for Walt Bellamy, a journeyman center. In a recent interview, Schaus said he wanted to acquire Bellamy but couldn't recall ever thinking about trading West. Whether or not he was on the block, West believed he was, and the pain

of that stays with him.

"To this day, that's the one thing that really rankles me," West said. "After giving everything I had in college for him [Schaus] and at the Lakers, it was a real slap in my face. I almost wish I had been traded because I would have had an opportunity to come back and play against this team, which always gives you some sort of tremendous emotional lift."

The incident colors his approach to managing his roster. "The most difficult thing of all is trading and removing players from your roster," he said. "It's simply no fun."

But it also left him prepared to deal with James Worthy after the much-publicized debate over his proposed trade to Dallas in 1986. "I had a talk

with him after it was said and done," West said, "and I told him that it was part of the business. He was hurt by it because he'd basically done everything that was asked of him here as a player."

Still, moving players is a major part of the business, and West has been fearless when he sees a deal that he thinks will make the team better.

3) He maintains a belief that the backcourt is the alpha and omega of basketball.

"I think guards have to do more things than every other player on the court," he said. "They're the first line of everything and the last line of everything, except defense. The center is the last line on defense. If you don't have good guards, you can't win. I don't care how good your people are up front. All you have to do is look at the NBA today, at the teams. You can be very good up front, and without the guards you still don't win.

"I love to have great centers. I love to play with them. But the most frustrating thing in the world is not to have someone competent playing with you as a guard."

4) The NBA is a players' game, and coaching is secondary to player talent.

West played for four different coaches in his 14 years with the Lakers. The nature of the game requires turnover, he explained. "When a coach has been around a few years, you've heard all of his stories, and frankly, it wears out."

The game today is overcoached, as compared to when he played, he says. "Basketball was a lot more simple then. The coaches coached. But today the coaches have way too much control. I don't feel they let the players play enough today. You've got wonderful players and you harness them by making them stand on their X's and O's and not letting them be a little more flexible. I think you see better play if you allow them more freedom."

Teams today are over-prepared, he said. But he admits that coaches spend so much time preparing out of fear that they'll be criticized and fired if they don't.

The irony is that as a GM, West is as prepared as they come. He spends much of his time scouting both college and pro games searching for talent.

"If I screw up, I want everyone to blame me and not our scouts," he explains.

Screwing up is less of a factor with West than most GMs, Schaus says, because he has such an eye for talent. Even as a young player, West could identify high school prospects for their West Virginia team, Schaus said. "He could see things other people couldn't."

FINDING THE NEXT MAGIC

"Maybe I'm spoiled," West says. "Maybe the success of this team has spoiled me a little bit. I try to be objective. I look at our record, and it makes no sense that I'm not happy. I should be happy. The reason I tend not to be happy is goal setting. You want to stretch yourself. You want to stretch your players and make them try to take that last step, and that's to end their season with a win. If you do that, you're gonna have a fun summer."

Because of that goal, West wouldn't ease his pain even if he could. He has suffered from ulcers and sleepless nights the last few seasons, particularly after games, when he twists and turns, running back every play in his mind. At the end of the 1989 season, a spot mysteriously appeared on his lung, frightening West and his family. It later went away, but doctors weren't sure what it was. The fear made him appreciate his family more, but it didn't dull his drive to keep "stretching."

"I hope these things stay with me," West says of his anxieties. "If I weren't like this, I probably wouldn't work."

After all, West *is* the Lakers, as Scott Ostler of *The National* pointed out last winter. "He is the lone thread that runs through the franchise's history from the first day in Los Angeles to this day. He was a rookie when the Lakers moved to L.A. from Minneapolis."

West, it seems, is constantly mindful of his burden of "being" the Lakers. "Since I came here in 1960," he said. "the Lakers have always had one or two players that have been at the top of the league in talent. In perpetuating this franchise, our next move is, where do we find another one of those guys?"

Most people are lucky, he says, to have one Magic Johnson in a lifetime. But West is obsessed with finding the next great one, "that one unique player who can get through the tough losses and come back and compete the next night. Those players are rare in this league. They'll play hard every night. They'll play in every building. They'll play in every circumstance. That kind of person is the most difficult to find."

Seeing the athletic talent is easy, he says. The hard part is identifying what can't be seen. He knows this will be nearly impossible, particularly when he didn't see it in Magic the first time around. But then no one really did.

"I felt he would be a very good player," West said of Johnson. "I had no idea he would get to this level. No idea. But, see, you don't know what's inside of people. You can see what they can do physically on the court. The things you could see about Magic, you loved. But you wondered where he was gonna play in the NBA. But he has just willed himself through hard work to take his game to another level. I don't think anyone knew he had that kind of greatness in him "

Yet identifying that player is just the first part of the task. Then West must manipulate the NBA's byzantine personnel structure so that the Lakers get the rights to him. That has become nearly impossible with the league's salary cap and expansion. Added to all that is the job of managing the Lakers' roster and keeping it young and competitive.

"The problem is, it's like a poker game," he says. "Any team that has a player play 10 years is probably going to be out of chips pretty soon. So you have to try like crazy within the scope of this league to keep your team young and productive. In the past, we've been able to bring in younger players and phase out older players at the end of their careers. That's where we are again. Are we willing to take a chance on keeping guys who maybe have four or five years left in their careers?"

The more he talks, the more he sounds like one Arnold Jacob Auerbach. It's not a comparison that offends West. He has long admired the Celtics' legendary president.

Asked if in the year 2010, at age 72, he'll still be managing the Lakers, West looks startled. That would depend on whether ownership thinks he's doing a good job, he says with a smile. "I do think this job is wearing. There's a lot of pressure on you. Maybe somewhere along the way a lesser role would be good for me. But again, I like to be active. I like to try to contribute. If I can't, then I shouldn't be here.

"The bottom line is, my number one priority in life is to see this franchise prosper. That's my life. It goes beyond being paid. It's something that's been a great source of pride. I would like people to know that I do care. It's not a self-interest thing. I do care about the winning and the perpetuation of the franchise. That's the one thing I care most about. I don't care about the pelts and the tributes. I like to work in my own weird way, working toward one goal, that's a winning team here."

Having heard all of that from Jerry West, you still wish there was a Field of Dreams out there for him.

Ease his pain.

His only salve, of course, would be another Laker championship. Yet even that wouldn't make him happy forever. But it would mean a win to end the season, and that in turn would make for a fun summer.

And that's about all that Jerry West, the man who has everything, has ever asked for.

Laker Profiles

VLADE DIVAC　　　　　#12

Height: 7-1
Weight: 248
Position: Center
Born: February 2, 1968 (Prijepolje, Yugoslavia)
High School: Kraljevo (Yugoslavia)
Residence: Marina del Rey

Selected by the Lakers in the first round of the 1989 college draft (26th overall).

1989-90: Vlade was one of the Lakers' pleasant surprises this season, showing a solid all-around game highlighted by excellent ball handling skills, shooting touch and quickness for a 7'1" center...named to the NBA's 1990 All-Rookie team...averaged 8.5 points and 6.2 rebounds in 19.6 minutes per game...along with A.C. Green was the only player to have appeared in all 82 of the Lakers games, starting in five of those games...finished seventh on the club in scoring (701), fourth in rebounds (512), third in steals (79)...led the Lakers in blocked shots with 114 (1.4), leading in that category in 41 games...shot .499 from the field, the club's fifth-best, and .708 from the free throw line...recorded season-high 25 points vs. Sacramento Jan. 15...grabbed season-high 14 rebounds Jan. 7 vs. Miami...shot in double figures in 35 games and rebounded in double figures in 13 games, recording nine double-doubles...averaged 9.1 points in nine post-season contests, shooting a team-high .727 FGs (32-44) and team-high .895 FTs (17-19)...was fourth on the club in rebounds in the playoffs with 5.3 per game, first in blocked shots with 1.7 per game...started at center in final post-season game vs. Phoenix, getting 10 points, 8 rebounds, and 3 steals...best playoff effort was Game 4 of the Western Conference first round, when he recorded 18 points and 6 rebounds.

CAREER: Vlade was the Lakers' first, and only, selection in the 1989 college draft...though only 21 at the time he had already played five years of pro ball in the top league in Yugoslavia...grew up in Prijepolje, in the republic of Serbia, and left his home at the age 12 to pursue a basketball career...moved to the town of Kraljevo, where he attended school and played for the club team...when he was 16 he signed with Sloga, his first pro team, where he played for two years...spent his last three campaigns with Partizan, and averaged approximately 20 points and 11 rebounds and hit 60 percent of his shots in his five pro seasons...has extensive interna-

tional experience...led the Yugoslavian Junior Olyumpic team to a gold-medal finish in the 1985 World University Games...played for the national team since the 1986 World Championships, where Yugoslavia captured the bronze medal...averaged 11.7 points and 6.5 rebounds in the 1988 Olympics as Yugoslavia took the silver medal...played against the Boston Celtics in the 1988 McDonald's Open in Madrid, getting nine points and eight rebounds...named to the 1988 Yugoslavian All-Star team by sportswriters there...Partizan won the European club championship that year.

PERSONAL: Vlade was drafted on June 27, 1989 and married in Yugoslavia four days later...over 1,000 people attended the wedding, which was televised nationally for an hour...arrived in LA on August 5 and signed with the club two days later...competed in four games for the Lakers' entry in the Southern California Summer Pro League that summer...posted double-doubles in all four games averaging 16.8 points and 16.0 rebounds...had Summer League-highs of 20 points and 20 rebounds, though not in the same game...following the Summer League he participated in two, one-week sessions of Pete Newell's heralded "Big Man" Camp...also played at UCLA each afternoon with many local NBA players...this past summer Vlade was the starting center for the Yugoslavian national team in the World Championships played in Argentina...in eight games, Vlade averaged 8.8 points, 5.2 rebounds, and 1.8 blocked shots...his rebounds and blocked shots were a team-high, and he was second in assists...ironically, Vlade is not the first Yugoslav player to be drafted by the Lakers: Kresimer Cosic of Brigham Young University, presently the coach of the Yugoslavian national team, was the club's fifth-round choice in 1973...Vlade's eating preference is steak...hobbies include going to the movies and walking...likes rock and roll and one of the first things he wanted to know upon arriving in LA was when were the Rolling Stones coming to town...his name is pronounced, Vla-day Dee-vatz, and his wife's is Sne-zuh-nah...fortunately, she prefers to be called Ana...Vlade and Snezana reside in Marina del Rey.

VLADE'S TOP CAREER PERFORMANCE

SCORING	REBOUNDS
1. 25 vs Sacramento (1-15-90)	1. 14 vs Miami (1-07-90)
2. 23 @ Denver (2-21-90)	2. 13 @ Orlando (12-10-89)
3. 21 vs Miami (1-07-90)	3. 13 @ Charlotte (12-12-89)
4. 21 vs Dallas (4-09-90)	4. 13 vs Houston (4-15-90)
5. 17 vs Washington (11-19-89)	5. 12 vs Seattle (3-25-90)

NBA REGULAR SEASON

SEASON	TEAM	G	MIN	FGM-FGA	PCT	3-PT	FTM-FTA	PCT	OFF	DEF	TOT	AST	PF-DQ	ST	BS	PTS	AVG
1989-90	LA	82	1611	274-549	.499	0-5	153-216	.708	167	345	512	75	240-279	110	114	701	8.5

PLAYOFFS

SEASON	TEAM	G	MIN	FGM-FGA	PCT	3-PT	FTM-FTA	PCT	OFF	DEF	TOT	AST	PF-DQ	ST	BS	PTS	AVG
1989-90	LA	9	175	32-44	.727	1-2	17-19	.895	16	32	48	10	27-18	13	15	82	9.1

LARRY DREW   #10

Height: 6-2
Weight: 190
Position: Guard
Born: April 2, 1958 (Kansas City, Kansas)
High School: Wyandotte (Kansas City)
College: Missouri '80
Residence: Inglewood

Signed with the Lakers as a veteran free agent on August 4, 1989.

1989-90: Larry proved to be a valuable acquisition for the Lakers last season, giving Earvin Johnson excellent support as back-up point guard...averaged 5.2 points and 2.7 assists in 16.6 minutes, scoring in double-figures in ten games...season-high of 15 points came vs. Dallas November 12...was second on the club in 3FGs (.395)...averaged 1.7 points in 7.3 minutes in seven post-season contests for the Lakers.

CAREER: Larry was a first-round draft choice of the Detroit Pistons in 1980, the 17th player selected overall...appeared in 76 games as a rookie with the Pistons, averaging 6.6 points...the arrival of Isiah Thomas to an already-crowded backcourt enabled the Pistons to trade him to Kansas City prior to his second season (August 26, 1981) for second-round picks in 1982 and 1984...appeared in 81 of 82 games in his first season in Kansas City (1981-82) and had his best season as a pro the following year, averaging a career-high 20.1 points and 8.1 assists...led the Kings in scoring and assists in 1982-83, and in assists again the following season...had four of the five, 30-point games in his career during the '82-83 campaign...had his career highs of 33 points vs. Houston on Jan. 21, 1983, 17 assists vs. Portland Nov. 28, 1984...played in 376 games in his five seasons with the Kings, averaging 14.7 points and 6.4 assists...averaged 8 points and 4.2 assists in his six career playoff games, all with the Kings...ranks fourth on the Kings' all-time list for steals, fifth in assists...traded to

the LA Clippers on Aug. 19, 1986 with Mike Woodson, a first-round draft choice in 1988 and a second-round pick in 1989 in exchange for Derek Smith, Franklin Edwards and Junior Bridgeman...averaged 12.4 points and 5.4 assists in 60 games with the Clippers in 1986-87, missing 20 games due to injuries and illness...averaged 10.3 points and a team-leading 5.2 assists in 74 games, 51 as a starter, in 1987-88...Larry opted to play with Scavollini Pesaro of the Italian League in 1988-89...averaged approximately 23 points and 5 assists as his team won the league title...Scavollini Pesaro also competed in the McDonald's Open in Madrid that year...in his previous eight NBA seasons prior to the Lakers, his teams have had one winning season, and have made two, three-game playoff appearances, losing all six of those games.

COLLEGE: Larry was an All-Big Eight and honorable mention All-America selection at Missouri...had a school-record 104 consecutive starts and finished as the school's all-time leader in assists and No. 2 scorer...started 114 of his 117 college outings and averaged 12.0 points over his collegiate career...averaged his college-high 15.2 points as a junior.

PERSONAL: Larry and his wife Sharon gave birth to their first child March 5, 1990, a baby boy, Larry Donnell II...the fifth of six children, Larry lists his mother as the person he most admires and his family as his most important possession...hobbies include music, fishing and visiting amusement parks...likes Mexican and Italian food...Larry and his wife, Sharon, live in Inglewood near his place of employment.

LARRY'S TOP CAREER PERFORMANCES

SCORING
1. 33 vs Houston (1-21-83)
2. 32 vs Houston @ St. Louis (2-16-83)
3. 32 @ Denver (4-17-83)
4. 31 vs New Jersey (12-15-82)
5. 30 vs Denver (3-7-84)

ASSISTS
1. 17 vs Portland (11-28-83)

NBA REGULAR SEASON

SEASON	TEAM	G	MIN	FGM-FGA	PCT	3-PT	FTM-FTA	PCT	OFF	DEF	TOT	AST	PF-DQ	ST	BS	PTS	AVG
1980-81	Det	76	1581	197-484	.407	4-17	106-133	.797	24	96	120	249	125-0	88	7	504	6.6
1981-82	KC	81	1973	358-757	.473	8-27	150-189	.794	30	119	149	419	150-0	110	1	874	10.8
1982-83	KC	75	2690	599-1218	.492	2-16	310-378	.820	44	163	207	610	207-1	125	10	1510	20.1
1983-84	KC	73	2363	474-1026	.462	3-10	243-313	.776	33	113	146	558	170-0	121	10	1194	16.4
1984-85	KC	72	2373	457-913	.501	7-28	154-194	.794	39	125	164	484	147-0	93	8	1075	14.9
1985-86	Sac	75	1971	376-776	.485	10-31	128-161	.795	25	100	125	338	134-0	66	2	890	11.9
1986-87	LAC	60	1566	295-683	.432	12-72	139-166	.837	26	77	103	326	107-0	60	2	741	12.4
1987-88	LAC	74	2024	328-720	.456	26-90	83-108	.769	21	98	119	383	114-0	65	0	765	10.3
1989-90	LA	80	1333	170-383	.444	32-81	46-60	.767	12	86	98	217	92-0	47	4	418	5.2
Totals		666	17874	3254-6960	.468	104-372	1359-1702	.799	254	977	1231	3584	1246-1	776	44	7971	12.0

PLAYOFFS

SEASON	TEAM	G	MIN	FGM-FGA	PCT	3-PT	FTM-FTA	PCT	OFF	DEF	TOT	AST	PF-DQ	ST	BS	PTS	AVG
1983-84	KC	3	70	7-19	.368	—	3-3	1.000	0	4	4	11	5-0	3	0	17	5.7
1986-86	Sac	3	56	14-25	.560	1-3	2-2	1.000	0	1	1	14	2-0	5	0	31	10.3
1989-90	LA	7	51	3-8	.375	1-4	5-6	.833	0	2	2	4	9-0	3	0	12	1.7
Totals		13	177	24-52	.462	2-7	10-11	.910	0	7	7	29	16-0	11	0	60	4.6

A.C. GREEN　　　　　　　#45

Height: 6-9
Weight: 224
Position: Forward
Born: October 4, 1963 (Portland)
High School: Benson Tech (Portland)
College: Oregon State '85
Residence: Los Angeles

Selected by the Lakers in the first round of the 1985 college draft (23rd overall).

1989-90: A.C. just missed career highs in both scoring and rebounding in 1989-90, averaging 12.9 points and 8.7 rebounds...had topped career highs in both categories every season he's been in the league prior to this season...was the Laker's leading rebounder for the fourth consecutive year, grabbing 712 total boards and leading the Lakers in that category in 39 of the 82 games...lone Laker to appear in all 82 games for the third year in a row, running his streak to 387 consecutive games played, including playoffs (321 regular season and 66 playoff)...has missed just three games in his five NBA seasons...shot .478 from the field (385-806), his career low, and .751 from the free throw line (278-370)...hit thirteen 3FGs (13-46), after making five over his first four seasons...finished fourth on the team in scoring with high game (27 points) coming three times...tied his career and season-high 18 rebounds Jan. 6 at Golden State and April 8 at Denver (tying his 18-rebound performance Nov. 8, 1987)...scored in double-figures in 53 games, including 20 of last 33, tallying 20 or more points in 15 contests...rebounded in double figures 30 times, recording 27 double-doubles, including four in a row in April...grabbed career and team-high 11 offensive rebounds Jan. 6 at Golden State...voted by fans to the starting line-up of the Western Conference All-Star team for his first appearance in the classic, edging out Utah's Karl Malone...was held scoreless in that game, but grabbed 3 rebounds in 12 minutes...averaged his career-high 11.8 points and a team-leading 9.0 boards in the playoffs, averaging 12.5 points and 6.0 rebounds vs. Houston in the first round, and 11.2 points and team-high 11.8 rebounds vs. Phoenix in the Western Conference semifinals...posted his playoff-high rebounds (18) in Game 4 vs. the Suns...high for the Lakers in rebounds in four of the nine post-season contests.

CAREER: A.C. was the Lakers' first-round selection in the 1985 college draft, the 23rd player chosen overall...became the first Laker rookie since LeRoy Ellis in 1962-63 to appear in every game...set a club rookie record with 10 offensive boards at Phoenix March 1, a figure exceeded just five times in Laker history...had 17 points and 16 rebounds in his second pro game Oct. 29 at Dallas, getting 15 points and 12 boards in the second half of that game...had three double-doubles as a rookie...after appearing in all 82 regular-season games and each of the club's first nine playoff contests he sat out the entire Western Conference Final vs. Houston, all coaches decision...moved into the starting lineup in 1986-87 for the final 72 games of the season and led the club in rebounds averaging 7.8...suffered a torn ligament in his left thumb in the club's final pre-

season game which sidelined him for three games, the only games he's missed due to illness or injury since he began playing in high school...averaged 11.4 points and a team-leading 8.7 rebounds in 1987-88, the lone Laker to appear in all 82 contests...grabbed his career-high 18 rebounds vs. Houston Nov. 8, 1987...selected by NBA coaches to the league's All-Defensive second team in 1988-89, the only Lakers honored...once again the lone Laker to appear in all 82 games, his second consecutive year...recorded career-high 33 points at Seattle April 4, 1989...scored in double figures in a season-high eight straight games in March 1989...had career-high 17-21 FTs vs. Portland Feb. 16...passed for his pro-high (regular season or playoffs) of seven assists in Game 2 vs. Phoenix in '89 playoffs...ranks fourth on the club's all-time list for offensive rebounds (1,135), sixth in defensive boards (2,022), seventh in blocked shots (279), ninth in steals (366), and tenth in FG percentage (.514).

COLLEGE: A.C. was selected as Pac-10 Player of the Year as a junior and wound up his career as Oregon State's second-leading rebounder and third-leading scorer...only Steve Johnson and ex-Laker Mel Counts scored more points for the Beavers and only Counts grabbed more boards...third player in OSU history to hit better than 60 percent from the floor over his career, finishing at .601...as a senior he was a third-team All-America choice by AP and UPI, Region 8 Player of the Year and a unanimous All-Pac 10 choice for the second year in a row...finalist for the John Wooden Award as a senior, finishing eighth in the balloting...scored career-high 39 points vs. Stanford as a senior...ranked fourth in the NCAA in FG pct. as a junior, finishing behind Akeem Olajuwon, Bobby Lee Hurt and Patrick Ewing...All-Pac 10 as a sophomore and Pac-10 All-Rookie selection as a freshman...led the Beavers in rebounding in each of his last three college seasons.

PERSONAL: The initials, A.C., like his father's, do not stand for full names — his name is simply A.C. Green Jr....plans to pursue a career as a minister and frequently speaks to youth groups...earned Player of the Year, All-State, All-District and All-Metro (Portland) honors after averaging 26 points as a high school senior, leading Benson Tech to the state title...played in the prestigious Dapper Dan Classic after his senior year...stood 5-11 in ninth grade, 6-8 as a high school senior...hobbies include tennis, bowling, baseball, football, golf and eating frozen yogurt...majored in speech communications in college...MVP of the Southern California Summer Pro League in 1987 and led the loop in scoring and rebounding the year before...A.C. is single and lives in Los Angeles during the season, though he spends part of the summer in his native Portland.

A.C.'S TOP CAREER PERFORMANCES

SCORING		REBOUNDING	
1.	33 @ Seattle (4-4-89)	1.	18 vs Houston (11-8-87)
2.	28 vs Denver (11-27-87)	2.	17 vs San Antonio (3-20-87)
3.	27 @ Seattle (1-3-89)	3.	16 @ Dallas (10-29-85)
4.	26 vs Portland (12-18-86)	4.	16 @ Houston (12-21-86)
5.	25 @ Phoenix (1-30-87)	5.	16 @ Sacramento (12-23-86)
6.	25 @ Dallas (1-29-89)	6.	16 @ Portland (2-5-87)
7.	24 vs Seattle (3-4-87)	7.	16 vs Denver (11-27-87)
8.	24 vs Charlotte (1-27-89)	8.	16 @ Boston (12-16-88)
9.	24 @ Houston (1-31-89)	9.	15　　8 times
10.	24 vs Indiana (3-3-89)		

NBA REGULAR SEASON

SEASON	TEAM	G	MIN	FGM-FGA	PCT	3-PT	FTM-FTA	PCT	OFF	DEF	TOT	AST	PF-DQ	ST	TO	BS	PTS	AVG
1985-86	LA	82	1542	209-388	.539	1-6	102-167	.611	160	221	381	54	229-2	49	99	49	521	6.4
1986-87	LA	79	2240	316-587	.538	0-5	220-282	.780	210	405	615	84	171-0	70	102	80	852	10.8
1987-88	LA	82	2636	322-640	.503	0-2	293-379	.773	245	465	710	93	204-0	87	120	45	937	11.4
1988-89	LA	82	2510	401-758	.529	4-17	282-359	.786	258	481	739	103	172-0	94	119	55	1088	13.3
1989-90	LA	82	2709	385-806	.478	13-46	278-370	.751	262	450	712	90	207-0	66	116	50	1061	12.9
Totals		407	11637	1633-3179	.514	18-66	1175-1557	.755	1135	2022	3157	424	983-2	366	556	279	4459	11.0

PLAYOFFS

SEASON	TEAM	G	MIN	FGM-FGA	PCT	3-PT	FTM-FTA	PCT	OFF	DEF	TOT	AST	PF-DQ	ST	TO	BS	PTS	AVG
1985-86	LA	9	106	9-17	.529	0-0	4-9	.444	3	13	16	0	13-0	1	4	3	22	2.4
1986-87	LA	18	505	71-130	.546	0-0	65-87	.747	54	88	142	11	47-0	9	17	8	207	11.5
1987-88	LA	24	726	92-169	.544	0-0	55-73	.753	57	118	175	20	61-0	11	26	12	239	10.0
1988-89	LA	15	502	47-114	.412	0-3	58-76	.763	38	99	137	18	37-1	16	23	6	152	10.1
1989-90	LA	9	252	41-79	.519	0-0	24-32	.750	34	47	81	9	22-0	5	14	4	106	11.8
Totals		75	2091	260-509	.511	0-3	206-277	.744	186	365	551	58	180-1	42	84	33	726	9.7

EARVIN JOHNSON   #32

Height: 6-9
Weight: 220
Position: Guard
Born: August 14, 1959 (Lansing, Michigan)
High School: Everett (Lansing)
College: Michigan State '81
Residence: Los Angeles

Selected by the Lakers in the first round of the 1979 college draft (first overall).

1989-90: For the second straight season and the third time in four years, Earvin was presented the NBA Most Valuable Player Award, the sixth player in NBA history to win the league's MVP two or more years in a row...earned first-team All-NBA status for the eighth year in a row...led the Lakers in scoring with 22.3 points per game, his third-highest scoring average of his career, finishing 18th in scoring in the league...ranked second in the NBA in assists with 11.5 per game and seventh in free throw percentage at .890...collected a league-high 11 triple-doubles in 1989-90 to push his career total to 123...shot .480 FGs (546-1138), a career-low, and .890 FTs...hit a career-high 106 3FGs this year, after making 117 total 3FGs in all ten previous seasons combined...set new career-highs for 3FGs-made and attempted April 21...besides scoring, also led the club in assists and steals (1.7), and was third in rebounds (6.7)...had season-high 38 points Marvh 9 vs. Dallas...FTs-made (19) and FTs-attempted (22) that game were new career highs...set Laker single-game assist record this year with 24 vs. Denver Nov. 17...tied record Jan. 9 at Phoenix...the previous record had been 23 by Johnson in 1984 and 1988, and also by Jerry West in 1967...led the Lakers in assists in all but six games he played in...rebounded in double-figures in 18 games, 20 or more points in 51 games, 30 or more points in 14 games, and had double-figure assists in 50 games, including 14 of the last 26...named the NBA's Edge Player of the month for the month of Feb., named Player of the Week for the period ending April 15...received his first NBA All-Star Game MVP on Feb. 11 in Miami (22p, 6r, 4a), his ninth All-Star appearance...missed three games this season, one due to an ankle sprain, one due to the flu and one DNP-CD in the season-finale at Portland...the Lakers are 63-44 in the 107 games he's missed in his career (63-45 including playoffs)...averaged a team-high 25.2 points and 12.8 assists in the nine playoff contests in 1990, appearing in his 11th straight post-season campaign...his rebounds (6.3) were the club's second-best effort...recorded his career playoff-high 43 points in both Game 4 and Game 5 vs. Phoenix.

CAREER: The Lakers made Earvin the first player selected in the 1979 college draft, using a pick the club acquired as compensation when Gail Goodrich signed as a free agent with the Jazz prior to the 1976-77 season...was first rookie in NBA history to be named MVP of the Finals after getting 42 points, 15 rebounds and seven assists while starting at center replacing the injured (sprained ankle) Kareem Abdul-Jabbar to lead the Lakers past Philadelphia in the sixth and final game of the 1980 NBA Finals...owns numerous Laker rookie records including assists (563), steals (187) and FT pct. (.810)...became the third rookie in club history to score 1,000 points...became the first rookie to start in the All-Star Game since Elvin Hayes in 1969...unanimous member of the All-Rookie team and runner-up to Larry Bird in the Rookie of the Year voting...became the third player to have won NCAA and NBA titles back-to-back joining Bill Russell and Henry Bibby, and Billy Thompson became the fourth in 1986-87...missed 45 games during his sophomore campaign due to torn cartilage in his left knee, though he averaged 21.6 points...returned from that injury on Feb. 27 and averaged 22.4 points and nine rebounds, sinking 54 percent of his FGs over the final 16 games...won his second playoff MVP award in three years as the Lakers captured another title in 1982...joined Oscar Robertson

and Wilt Chamberlain as the third player to record 700 points, rebounds and assists that season...led the league in steals (2.67) for the second year in a row and placed second in assists (9.5)...had 18 double-doubles that year...set a club record with 13 offensive rebounds at Houston in 1981-82...1982-83 marked the first year he was selected to the All-NBA first team and he's been a fixture on the team ever since...led the league in assists that season (10.5)...broke Jerry West's club record with 829 assists that season, and he's improved the record in five of the seven seasons since...in 1983-84 he was the inaugural winner of the Schick Pivotal Player Award, top vote-getter on The Sporting News All-NBA team (voted by the players) and first team All-NBA again...led the league in assists with an NBA-record 13.1, and set an NBA playoff record with 24 assists vs. Phoenix in the Western Conference final...had 968 assists in 1984-85, the third-highest total in NBA history at that time, though he did not lead the league...led the league in assists for the third time in 1985-86, averaging 12.6...handed out his 5,000th career assist March 13, 1986 vs. Seattle...became first player to receive more than 1 million votes in the 1986 All-Star balloting...had his greatest season in 1986-87, joining Willis Reed, Moses Malone and Larry Bird as the only players to be named NBA MVP of the regular season and NBA Finals in the same season (NBA Finals MVP was first awarded in 1969)...became first player to win the Finals MVP award for a third time, having done so in 1980 and 1982...the only other guards to win MVP were Oscar Roberston in 1963-64 and Bob Cousy in 1956-57...voted to All-NBA first team for the fifth year in a row and the lone unanimous selection...led the Lakers in scoring for the first time in his career, averaging a career-high 23.9 points to rank 10th in the league...still led the league in assists, amassing a club-record 977 feeds...named NBA Player of the Week an unprecedented five times, and scored his career-high 46 points in an OT win at Sacramento on Dec. 23...had triple-doubles in four consecutive games for the first time in his career...scored his 10,000th point at Portland Feb. 5, 1987...became all-time leader in assists in All-Star Game competition...knocked out of action by a late-season groin injury for 19 games in 1987-88...averaged 19.6 points and 11.9 assists to rank second in the league...failed to shoot 50 percent FGs for the first time in his career finishing at .492...season highlight was his buzzer-beating bank shot from 20 feet, lifting Lakers to a 115-114 win in Boston Dec. 11, initiating the club's 15-game winning streak...had three dreams fulfilled in the 1988 NBA Final vs. Detroit: he got to play for a Championship in front of his father for the first time, he got to play for a title in his hometown for the first time, and he played for back-to-back championship teams...in 1989, he was presented with his second NBA MVP award and earned first-team All-NBA status for the seventh year in a row...midway through Game 2 of the NBA Finals, however, he injured his left hamstring and was forced to join Byron Scott on the sideline as Detroit ended the Lakers' hopes for a third straight championship...when he sat out Game 4 of the Finals, it was the first playoff game he missed in his career...had his second-highest scoring average for a season (22.5) and became the first Laker to lead the NBA in FT pct (a career-best .911, a club record)...recorded 17 triple-doubles and missed seven others by one rebound...hit 59 3FGs, one more than he made in his first nine seasons combined...decided three games with last-second heroics, against Phoenix, Denver, and Washington...missed five games in 1988-89, not including the All-Star Game, due to a partially torn left hamstring suffered Feb. 8 against Golden State...ranks second on the NBA's all-time assist list, trailing Oscar Robertson by a 9,887-8,932 margin...ranks third with 1,596 steals...among active NBA players he's first in assists, second in steals, fourth in FTM and FTA...begins the season ranked 42nd in scoring in NBA history with 15,708 points...on the Lakers' all-time regular-season chart he's first in assists (total and average) and steals, second in offensive and defensive rebounds, fourth in points, minutes, FGM and FTM-FTA, fifth in games, scoring average, blocks, rebounds and FGA...on the NBA's all-time playoff list he's first in assists and steals, third in FTM, fifth in games, sixth in FTA and minutes, eighth in 3FGA, and ninth in FGM...on the Lakers' all-time playoff list he's the leader in assists and steals, third in games and fourth in rebounds and points.

COLLEGE: Led Michigan State to a 25-5 record as a freshman as the Spartans won their first Big Ten title in 19 years...MSU went 26-6 his sophomore year and won the NCAA Tournament, beating Indiana State and Larry Bird in the final...named Final Four MVP that year, his first of three titles and post-season MVP awards in a four-year span that included his first three pro seasons...selected by the Lakers as the number one pick in the NBA draft following his sophomore year.

PERSONAL: Earvin had a busy summer, spending part of it conducting his basketball camps and speaking at various others around the country...also played in a variety of charity All-Star Games, including those sponsored by Larry Bird, Isiah Thomas and Dominique Wilkins...conducted his fifth annual all-star game/black-tie dinner "A Mid-Summer Night's Magic", benefiting the United Negro College Fund raising $1 million, bringing the five-year total near $5 million...became a partner in a lucrative Pepsi bottling company in Washington, D.C....chaired a three-on-three basketball tournament in the GW Forum's parking lot, and even found time to return home to Lansing to play in a MSU/U-M reunion game...named Athlete of the Decade by Sport Magazine...voted American Express/NBA Man of the Year for 1986-87 by the fans for his charity and community service work...voted to the NBA's official All-Interview first team the past four years...he and Larry Bird were the first athletes to appear in a rock video, Loverboy's "Working For The Weekend", in 1986...has numerous nationwide endorsements and actively involved with several charities, including a program for students with reading disabilities in Lansing...avid softball player and a rabid baseball and football fan...his autobiography, "Magic", was published in the spring of 1983...plans to return to school to finish the requirements for the communications degree he put on hold when he left school to join the NBA after his sophomore year...Earvin received his nickname "Magic" from a Lansing sportswriter after a 36-point, 18-rebound, 16-assist performance in high school...Earvin is single and lives in Los Angeles and has a son, Andre, who lives in Lansing.

EARVIN'S TOP CAREER PERFORMANCES

SCORING	REBOUNDING	ASSISTS
1. 46 @ Sacramento (12-23-86)	1. 18 vs Chicago (3-7-80)	1. 23 vs Seattle (2-21-84)
2. 42 @ New Jersey (1-19-87)	2. 17 @ Atlanta (1-15-83)	2. 23 @ Dallas (4-20-88)
3. 41 @ Utah (3-28-81)	3. 17 @ Denver (4-1-89)	3. 22 vs Cleveland (11-17-83)
4. 40 @ Detroit (1-9-82)	4. 17 vs Denver (4-18-89)	4. 21 @ Atlanta (1-15-83)
5. 40 vs Indiana (2-13-87)	5. 16 @ Kansas City (3-5-80)	5. 21 @ LA Clippers (12-6-88)
6. 40 vs Seattle (11-30-88)	6. 16 vs Portland (3-12-80)	6. 21 vs Seattle (4-23-89)
7. 39 vs Portland (4-7-85)	7. 16 vs Cleveland (11-11-80)	7. 20 @ Philadelphia (1-5-83)
8. 39 vs Boston (2-15-87)	8. 16 vs San Antonio (3-10-81)	8. 20 vs Milwaukee (1-26-83)
9. 39 vs Houston (1-18-88)	9. 16 @ Denver (1-19-82)	9. 20 vs San Diego (3-9-83)
10. 38 @ Houston (12-21-86)	10. 16 vs Detroit (1-22-82)	10. 20 vs New Jersey (11-25-83)
11. 38 @ Golden State (1-10-87)	11. 16 vs Houston (3-21-82)	11. 20 @ Atlanta (12-18-84)
	12. 16 @ Denver (3-31-83)	12. 20 @ Houston (12-19-84)
	13. 16 vs Seattle (11-29-85)	13. 20 vs LA Clippers (11-20-85)
		14. 20 vs Phoenix (12-12-85)
		15. 20 @ Houston (4-6-86)
		16. 20 vs Denver (3-20-87)

NBA REGULAR SEASON

SEASON	TEAM	G	MIN	FGM-FGA	PCT	3-PT	FTM-FTA	PCT	OFF	DEF	TOT	AST	PF-DQ	ST	TO	BS	PTS	AVG
1979-80	LA	77	2795	503-949	.530	7-31	374-462	.810	166	430	596	563	218-1	197	305	41	1387	18.0
1980-81	LA	37	1371	312-587	.531	3-17	171-225	.760	101	219	320	317	100-0	127	143	27	798	21.6
1981-82	LA	78	2991	556-1036	.537	6-29	329-433	.760	252	499	751	743	223-1	208	286	34	1447	18.6
1982-83	LA	79	2907	511-933	.548	0-21	304-380	.800	214	469	683	829	200-1	176	301	47	1326	16.8
1983-84	LA	67	2567	441-780	.565	6-29	290-358	.810	99	392	491	875	169-1	150	306	49	1178	17.6
1984-85	LA	77	2781	504-899	.561	7-37	391-464	.843	90	386	476	968	155-0	113	305	25	1406	18.3
1985-86	LA	72	2578	483-918	.526	10-43	378-434	.871	85	341	426	907	133-0	113	273	16	1354	18.8
1986-87	LA	80	2904	683-1308	.522	8-39	535-631	.848	122	382	504	977	168-0	138	300	36	1909	23.9
1987-88	LA	72	2637	490-996	.492	11-56	417-489	.853	88	361	449	858	147-0	114	269	13	1408	19.6
1988-89	LA	77	2886	579-1137	.509	59-188	513-563	.911	111	496	607	988	172-0	138	312	22	1730	22.5
1989-90	LA	79	2937	546-1138	.480	106-276	567-637	.890	128	394	522	907	167-1	132	289	34	1765	22.3
Totals		795	29354	5608-10680	.525	223-766	4269-5076	.841	1456	4369	5825	8932	1852-5	1596	3089	344	15708	19.8

PLAYOFFS

SEASON	TEAM	G	MIN	FGM-FGA	PCT	3-PT	FTM-FTA	PCT	OFF	DEF	TOT	AST	PF-DQ	ST	TO	BS	PTS	AVG
1979-80	LA	16	658	103-199	.518	2-8	85-106	.802	52	116	168	151	47-1	49	65	6	293	18.3
1980-81	LA	3	127	19-49	.388	0-0	13-20	.650	8	33	41	21	14-1	8	11	3	51	17.0
1981-82	LA	14	562	83-157	.529	0-4	77-93	.828	54	104	158	130	50-0	40	44	3	243	17.4
1982-83	LA	15	643	100-206	.485	0-11	68-81	.840	51	77	128	192	49-0	34	64	12	268	17.9
1983-84	LA	21	837	151-274	.551	0-7	80-100	.800	26	113	139	284	71-0	42	79	20	382	18.2
1984-85	LA	19	687	116-226	.513	1-7	100-118	.847	19	115	134	289	48-0	32	76	4	333	17.5
1985-86	LA	14	541	110-205	.537	0-11	82-107	.766	21	79	100	211	43-0	27	45	1	302	21.6
1986-87	LA	18	666	146-271	.539	2-10	98-118	.831	28	111	139	219	37-0	31	51	7	392	21.8
1987-88	LA	24	965	169-329	.514	7-14	132-155	.852	32	98	130	303	61-0	34	83	4	477	19.9
1988-89	LA	14	518	85-174	.489	10-35	78-86	.907	15	68	83	165	30-1	27	53	3	258	18.4
1989-90	LA	9	376	76-155	.490	5-23	70-79	.886	12	45	57	115	28-0	11	36	1	227	25.2
Totals		168	6580	1158-2245	.516	27-130	883-1063	.831	318	959	1277	2080	500-3	335	607	64	3226	19.2

BYRON SCOTT   #4

Height: 6-4
Weight: 193
Position: Guard
Born: March 28, 1961 (Ogden, Utah)
High School: Morningside (Inglewood)
College: Arizona State '83
Residence: Los Angeles

Acquired by the Lakers on October 10, 1983 along with Swen Nater from San Diego for Norm Nixon, Eddie Jordan and two draft choices.

1989-90: Byron averaged 15.5 points for the Lakers in 1989-90, placing him third on the club's scoring list for the second consecutive season...average was the lowest since he averaged 15.4 points in 1985-86...shot career-lows .470 from the field (472-1005) and .766 from the free throw line (160-209), but led the club in 3FGs, connecting on .423 of his shots (93-220), the league's fifth-best accuracy overall...scored in double figures in all but nine games, including 23 consecutive games, leading the Lakers in scoring in eleven games...scored 20 or more points on 19 occasions...was second on the team in assists with 274 (3.6), fourth in steals with 77 (1.0), and sixth in rebounds with 242 (3.1)...his six steals Jan. 10 vs. Orlando was a club season-high...missed five games due to injury, three straight games in March because of a minor strain of his left hamstring, the same hamstring originally injured during the NBA Finals in June '89...missed last two games of the season with a sprained left ankle...season-high scoring of 33 points (11-15 FGs) came Nov. 10 vs. Charlotte...had career-high 10 rebounds vs. Phoenix Nov. 7...hit game-winning 3-pointer at the buzzer in overtime Feb. 20 at San Antonio to give the Lakers a one-point victory...made at least one 3FG in 19 consecutive games midway through the season...was the Laker's third-leading scorer (13.4) in nine playoff games, hitting 46 percent FGs and 13-34 3FGs (.382)...averaged 13.8 points, 1.8 assists, and team-high 2.8 steals in the first round against Houston, hitting 21-45 FGs (.467) and 6-14 3FGs (.429)...had playoff high 18 points twice against Phoenix in Western Conference semifinals.

CAREER: Byron was the fourth player and first guard selected in the 1983 college draft, but was traded by the Clippers to the Lakers the day before the pre-season schedule started...after a slow start Byron worked his way into the starting lineup and wound up as the third-leading vote-getter on the All-Rookie team...was shooting just .364 FGs after his first 16 games but shot .509 after Jan. 1 to finish at .484...suffered a sprained right knee during the last week of the regular season which slowed him during the early rounds of the playoffs...shot his career-high .539 FGs in 1984-85 and led the NBA with a .433 3FG pct. that season, the highest since Campy Russell shot .439 in 1981-82...became first guard and joined Wilt Chamberlain, Mitch Kupchak and Kareem Abdul-Jabbar as only players in Laker history to hit 10 FGs without a miss when he shot 10-10 on Feb. 26, 1986...finished fourth in the NBA in both FT (.892) and 3FG (.436) percentage in 1986-87, establishing Laker club records in both categories...made his first appearance in the Long Distance Shootout during All-Star Weekend...had his best season in 1987-88, joining Elgin Baylor, Jerry West, Gail Goodrich, Kareem Abdul-Jabbar and Earvin Johnson as the only players to lead the Lakers in scoring over the last 30 years...ranked 12th in the NBA averaging a career-high 21.7 points...had his career-high 38 points Feb. 14, 1988 vs. Boston hitting 15-19 FGs...scored 30 or more 11 times after Dec. 15 that season after doing so in just eight games in his career prior to that...scored in double figures in last 64 games...in addition to having his best scoring year he registered career highs in assists, steals and blocks, and posted career highs in assists, steals, and blocks.

BYRON'S TOP CAREER PERFORMANCES

SCORING
1. 38 vs Boston (2-14-88)
2. 37 vs Philadelphia (12-29-87)
3. 35 @ Detroit (1-8-88)
4. 35 vs Dallas (3-12-88)
5. 35 vs Boston (2-19-88)
6. 35 vs San Antonio (3-30-89)
7. 33 @ Sacramento (12-23-86)
8. 33 @ Sacramento (2-20-89)
9. 33 vs Denver (11-9-88)
10. 32   4 times

ASSISTS
1. 10 vs Phoenix (11-20-84)
2. 10 vs Dallas (3-12-88)
3. 10 vs New Jersey (3-14-88)
4. 10 vs Denver (3-25-88)
5. 9 vs Golden State (10-30-84)
6. 9 @ Portland (4-3-87)
7. 9 vs Phoenix (12-15-87)
8. 9 vs Washington (2-23-88)
9. 9 vs Phoenix (4-15-88)
10. 8 @ Seattle (12-20-83)
11. 8 vs Denver (11-7-86)
12. 8 @ Atlanta (1-21-87)

NBA REGULAR SEASON

SEASON	TEAM	G	MIN	FGM-FGA	PCT	3-PT	FTM-FTA	PCT	OFF	DEF	TOT	AST	PF-DQ	ST	TO	BS	PTS	AVG
1983-84	LA	74	1637	334-690	.484	8-34	112-139	.806	50	114	164	176	174-0	81	116	19	788	10.6
1984-85	LA	81	2305	541-1003	.539	26-60	187-228	.820	57	153	210	244	197-1	100	138	17	1295	16.0
1985-86	LA	76	2190	507-989	.513	22-61	138-176	.784	55	134	189	164	167-0	85	110	15	1174	15.4
1986-87	LA	82	2729	554-1134	.489	65-149	224-251	.892	63	223	286	281	163-0	125	144	18	1387	17.0
1987-88	LA	81	3048	710-1348	.527	62-179	272-317	.858	76	257	333	335	204-2	155	161	27	1754	21.7
1988-89	LA	74	2605	588-1198	.491	77-193	195-226	.863	72	230	302	231	181-1	114	157	27	1448	19.6
1989-90	LA	77	2593	472-1005	.470	93-220	160-209	.766	51	191	242	274	180-2	77	122	31	1197	15.5
Totals		544	17107	3706-7367	.503	353-896	1288-1546	.833	424	1302	1726	1706	1986-6	737	948	154	9053	16.6

PLAYOFFS

SEASON	TEAM	G	MIN	FGM-FGA	PCT	3-PT	FTM-FTA	PCT	OFF	DEF	TOT	AST	PF-DQ	ST	TO	BS	PTS	AVG
1983-84	LA	20	404	74-161	.460	2-10	21-35	.600	11	26	37	34	39-1	18	26	2	171	8.6
1984-85	LA	19	585	138-267	.517	10-21	35-44	.795	16	36	52	50	47-0	41	24	4	321	16.9
1985-86	LA	14	470	90-181	.497	6-17	38-42	.905	15	400	55	42	38-0	19	30	2	224	16.0
1986-87	LA	18	608	103-210	.490	7-34	53-67	.791	20	42	62	57	52-0	19	25	4	266	14.8
1987-88	LA	24	897	178-357	.499	24-55	90-104	.865	26	74	100	60	65-0	34	47	5	470	19.6
1988-89	LA	11	402	79-160	.494	15-39	46-55	.836	10	35	45	25	31-0	18	20	2	219	19.9
1989-90	LA	9	325	49-106	.462	13-34	10-13	.769	7	30	37	23	32-1	20	13	3	121	13.4
Totals		115	3691	711-1442	.493	77-210	293-360	.814	105	283	388	291	304-2	169	185	22	1792	15.6

MYCHAL THOMPSON   #43

Height: 6-10
Weight: 235
Position: Center/Forward
Born: January 30, 1955 (Nassau, Bahamas)
High School: Jackson (Miami)
College: Minnesota '78
Residence: Los Angeles

Acquired by the Lakers on February 13, 1987 from San Antonio in exchange for Frank Brickowski, Petur Gudmundsson, a first-round pick in the 1987 draft, a second-round pick in the 1990 draft and cash.

1989-90: How does one possibly succeed a legend?...Mychal Thompson replaced Kareem Abdul-Jabbar as the Lakers' starting center, and responded with 10.1 points and 6.8 rebounds in 27.0 minutes per contest...starting all 70 games he appeared in during the regular season, Mychal finished sixth on the club in scoring and shot .500 from the field (281-562), the club's fourth best...also shot his Laker-high .706 from the free throw line (144-204)...scored in double figures 34 times, including six consecutive games in Feb...fifth on the club in rebounds, Mychal rebounded in double digits on 11 occasions, leading the Lakers on 17 occasions...recorded eight double-doubles...was second on the club in blocked shots with 73, leading the Lakers in 22 games...recorded Laker high for blocked shots in one game (5) at San Antonio Feb. 20...missed twelve games this season: eleven due to injury (6 - Achilles heel injury; 4 - hyperextended knee; 1 - sprained ankle), and one due to C-D...recorded season-high 24 points Feb. 6 at Portland and season-high 12 rebounds vs. Sacramento Jan. 15...his 11 defensive rebounds that night was his Laker career high...averaged 6.4 points and playoff-low 4.3 rebounds in the post-season, shooting .477 from the field and .615 from the line...high game was Game 1 vs. Houston in the first round: 12 points, 8 rebounds, 5 blocked shots.

CAREER: The Portland Trail Blazers made Mychal the first player selected in the 1978 college draft...played for Portland for seven years and sat out another season (1979-80) after suffering a broken left leg in the Bahamas in July, 1979....led the club in scoring once and in rebounding for four seasons, and remains the Blazers' all-time leader in minutes and rebounds...named to NBA All-Rookie team in 1978-79 after averaging 14.7 points and 8.3 rebounds...had 37 points in his second pro game October 17, 1981 vs. Kansas City, a figure he has topped only once in regular-season play, and had his career-high 22 rebounds in his ninth pro game November 3, 1978 vs. San Diego...sat out the entire following year, though, aside from that season, he's missed just 27 games in his 10 full campaigns...had his best season, statistically, in 1981-82, as he finished 17th in the league in scoring (20.8) and fourth in rebounding (11.7), both figures being his career highs...had his regular-season scoring high on December 11, 1981, at The Forum against the Lakers...he scored his pro career-high 40 points in the playoffs against Kansas City on April 3, 1981, a Blazer post-season record...Portland traded Mychal and the draft rights to Larry Krystkowiak to San Antonio in exchange for Steve Johnson on June 19, 1986...averaged 12.3 points and 5.6 rebounds in 49 outings with the Spurs before being dealt to the Lakers on Feb. 13, 1987, for Frank Brickowski, Petur Gudmundsson, a first-round pick in the 1987 draft (Greg Anderson), a second-round pick in the 1990 draft and cash...Lakers finished the regular season 28-5 after the trade...his first game with the club was a nationally-televised contest against Boston on Feb. 15 when, without the benefit of any

practice time with the club, he scored 10 points in 29 minutes, playing the final 20 minutes of the contest...his addition made the Lakers the first NBA club to have four No. 1 draft picks on its roster, as he joined Kareem Abdul-Jabbar, Earvin Johnson and James Worthy...prior to last season, had missed just four games over the previous four seasons...scored his 10,000th NBA point March 24, 1987 at Phoenix...Lakers' back-to-back title in 1988 gave Mychal an 8-0 mark in playoff series with the club...finished the 1987-88 season strongly and wound up as the club's leading scorer off the bench averaging 11.6...averaged 13.7 points and 7.8 rebounds with .541 FGs over the final two months of the season...had his three-year Laker highs of 28 points March 20 at Golden State, 13 rebounds twice...Lakers prevailed in first 11 playoff series he competed in with the club prior to 1988 loss to Detroit in NBA Finals...started eight games in 1988-89 in Kareem's absence and the club went 7-1 in those games as he averaged 13.6 points and 7.8 rebounds...Laker's top scorer (11.4) and rebounder (5.1) of the bench in the '89 playoffs, ranking fourth in both areas overall...acquired by Lakers from San Antonio on Feb. 13, 1987 and since then the Lakers are 209-69 (.752) in regular-season play, 254-90 (.738) including playoffs...has appeared in 66 playoff games in his four seasons with the Lakers after making just 30 post-season appearances in his first eight pro campaigns...enters this season ranked 89th on the league's all-time regular-season scoring chart with 12,522 points...Mychal's the 9th-leading rebounder among active NBA players with 6,723 boards...ranks ninth on the Lakers' all-time FG pct. chart at .516, 10th in offensive rebounds (575), and is the club's 8th-leading all-time shot-blocker (241).

COLLEGE: Mychal was a two-time All-America at Minnesota, where he finished as the school's all-time leader in scoring (1,992), rebounding (956) and field goal percentage (.561)...set school records as a sophomore with a 25.9 scoring average and a .606 field goal percentage...averaged 20.8 points over his four college campaigns: 12.5 as a freshman, 25.9 as a sophomore, 22.0 as a junior and 22.1 as a senior...hit at least 53 percent of his field goals each year.

PERSONAL: Mychal is a native of the Bahamas and has done some work for the Bahamas Department of Tourism...Mychal and his wife Julie had their second son, Klay Alexander, Feb. 8th...their first son, Mychel, turned two in June...his brother, Colin, played in the Dodgers' minor league system and another brother, Andy, works with NBA Entertainment...splits his time in the off season between Portland and Nassau...among his favorite Bahamian cuisine is the breakfast of boiled fish and Johnny cakes...enjoys playing golf...a fixture on the first two NBA All-Interview teams...played high school ball at Jackson High in Miami...studied business administration at Minnesota...TV addict and loves his soap operas...big fan of pro wrestling...voracious reader of NBA Notes columns and visits out-of-town newspaper stands in most NBA cities.

MYCHAL'S TOP CAREER PERFORMANCES

SCORING
1. 38 @ Lakers (12-11-81)
2. 37 vs Kansas City (10-17-78)
3. 37 @ Seattle (11-25-81)
4. 37 vs Milwaukee (3-23-82)
5. 33 vs Golden State (3-8-81)
6. 33 vs LA Clippers (2-26-85)
7. 32 @ Denver (11-8-84)
8. 31 @ Indiana (3-9-78)
9. 31 @ LA Clippers (11-3-84)
10. 31 vs LA Clippers (11-18-84)

REBOUNDING
1. 22 vs San Diego (11-3-78)
2. 21 @ Phoenix (12-10-81)
3. 21 @ Indiana (2-14-82)
4. 20 vs Phoenix (4-16-82)
5. 20 @ Seattle (12-21-82)
6. 19 vs Denver (11-8-81)
7. 19 vs San Diego (1-28-82)
8. 19 vs Utah (2-5-82)
9. 19 vs Seattle (4-18-82)

NBA REGULAR SEASON

Season	TEAM	G	MIN	FGM-FGA	PCT	3-PT	FTM-FTA	PCT	OFF	DEF	TOT	AST	PF-DQ	ST	BS	PTS	AVG
1978-79	Por	73	2144	460-938	.490	0-0	154-269	.572	198	406	604	176	270-10	67	134	1074	14.7
1980-81	Por	79	2790	569-1151	.494	0-1	207-323	.641	223	463	686	284	260-5	62	170	1345	17.0
1981-82	Por	79	3129	681-1303	.523	0-0	280-446	.628	258	663	921	319	233-2	69	107	1642	20.8
1982-83	Por	80	3017	505-1033	.489	0-1	249-401	.621	183	570	753	380	213-1	68	110	1259	15.7
1983-84	Por	79	2648	487-929	.524	0-2	266-399	.667	235	453	688	308	237-2	84	108	1240	15.7
1984-85	Por	79	2616	572-1111	.515	0-0	307-449	.684	211	407	618	205	216-0	78	104	1451	18.4
1985-86	Por	82	2569	503-1011	.498	0-0	198-309	.641	181	427	608	176	267-5	76	35	1204	14.7
1986-87	SA/LA	82	1890	359-797	.450	1-2	219-297	.737	138	274	412	115	202-1	45	71	938	11.4
1987-88	LA	80	2007	370-722	.512	0-3	185-292	.634	198	291	489	66	251-1	38	79	925	11.6
1988-89	LA	80	1994	291-521	.559	0-1	156-230	.678	157	310	467	48	224-0	58	59	738	9.2
1989-90	LA	70	1883	281-562	.500	0-0	144-204	.706	173	304	477	43	207-0	33	73	706	10.1
Totals		863	26687	5078-10078	.504	1-10	2365-3619	.653	2155	4568	6723	2120	2580-27	678	1050	12522	14.5

PLAYOFFS

Season	TEAM	G	MIN	FGM-FGA	PCT	3-PT	FTM-FTA	PCT	OFF	DEF	TOT	AST	PF-DQ	ST	BS	PTS	AVG
1978-79	Por	3	121	27-54	.500	0-0	5-10	.500	9	22	31	6	11-0	2	5	59	19.7
1980-81	Por	3	132	31-51	.608	0-0	13-18	.722	5	18	23	4	10-0	3	9	75	25.0
1982-83	Por	7	284	40-85	.471	0-0	25-38	.658	16	40	56	39	24-0	6	8	105	15.0
1983-84	Por	4	121	22-44	.500	0-0	17-22	.773	9	20	29	15	11-0	5	3	61	15.3
1984-85	Por	9	250	50-102	.490	0-0	33-49	.673	25	47	72	14	32-2	7	12	133	14.8
1985-86	Por	4	140	31-54	.574	0-0	14-26	.538	11	22	33	14	13-0	1	3	76	19.0
1986-87	LA	18	401	62-137	.453	0-0	34-50	.680	29	59	88	9	50-0	7	17	158	8.8
1987-88	LA	24	615	98-191	.513	0-0	36-62	.581	63	107	170	12	70-1	17	21	232	9.7

JAMES WORTHY   #42

Height: 6-9
Weight: 225
Position: Forward
Born: February 27, 1961 (Gastonia, North Carolina)
High School: Ashbrook (Gastonia)
College: North Carolina '83
Residence: Los Angeles

Selected by the Lakers in the first round (first overall) of the 1982 college draft.

1989-90: James finished this season as the club's second-leading scorer for the fifth consecutive year, averaging a career-high 21.1 points...ranked ninth in the NBA, second on the club, in FG pct this season (.548)...was second on the club in assists (288) and steals (99), and fourth in rebounds (478), rebounding in double-figures in seven games...led the Lakers in scoring in 31 games, scoring 20 or more points on 47 occasions and 30 or more points on nine occasions...prior to an 8-point performance vs. Cleveland in March, James had scored in double-figures in 77 consecutive regular-season games (92 including playoffs), with last game under 10 points coming in March 1989 at Miami...high game came vs. Suns in home opener Nov. 7 with 35 points...reached career milestone of 10,000 points vs. Indiana Nov. 15, the ninth Laker player to do so...recorded Laker's season-high FGM (16) Nov. 7 vs. Phoenix and FGA (27) Feb. 14 vs. Portland...missed only two games this season, March 20 vs. Charlotte due to back spasms and April 22 at Portland DNP-CD...started the year ranked 10th in NBA history in FG pct. with .556, finished ninth with .555...had eight double-doubles, while scored in single digits just one time...had his season-high 13 rebounds three times...recorded career-high 12 assists Jan. 24 at Indiana...sank .782 FTs for the second consecutive year, down slightly from his career-best mark of .796 in 1987-88...made his fifth straight All-Star Game appearance getting two points and four rebounds...averaged 24.2 points and 5.6 rebounds in the playoffs, shooting .526 FGs and .837 FTs, leading the Lakers in seven of the nine post-season games...led the Lakers in all four of the first round games vs. Houston, averaging a team-high 28.0 points for the series...high post-season game (34 points, 11 rebounds) came in Game 1 vs. Houston...this was the first time in four years that James was not the club's top point-maker in the playoffs.

CAREER: James became the first No. 1 draft pick to be selected by the reigning NBA Champions when the Lakers selected him in the first round of the 1982 college draft, using a pick obtained from the Cleveland Cavaliers...the Lakers acquired the pick and Butch Lee for Don Ford and a 1980 first-round choice (Chad Kinch) on February 15, 1980...he became the first North Carolina player ever drafted No. 1 and joined Earvin Johnson as the only No. 1 draft picks the Lakers have had since moving to Los Angeles...was a unanimous choice for the All-Rookie team after averaging 13.4 points to become the fourth rookie in Laker history to score 1,000 points....his .579 FG pct. topped all NBA rookies that year and remains a Laker rookie record...suffered a fractured tibia just below his left knee on April 10 and was sidelined for the playoffs...returned from the fractured leg to appear in all 82 games in 1983-84 and scoring average improved to 14.5 points...averaged 22.1 points in the Finals vs. Boston and set a Championship Series record by hitting 67-105 FGs (.638)...averaged 17.6 points and ranked sixth in the NBA in FG pct. (.572) in 1984-85...began wearing a pair of goggles similar to Kareem after suffering a laceration to the conjuctiva of his right eye at Utah March 13, 1985...scored in double figures in each of the club's 19 playoff games that year and averaged 21.5 points with .622 FGs as the

club won the title...set another NBA playoff record by hitting 49-68 FGs (.721) in the five-game Western Conference final vs. Denver...averaged 20 points per game for the first time in 1985-86, scoring an even 1,500 points in 75 contests...ranked fourth in the NBA with a .579 FG pct., matching his career high...had 20 points in his All-Star Game debut as a West starter...averaged 19.4 points during the 1986-87 regular season and led the club in the playoffs by averaging 23.6 points...started in the All-Star Game for the second year in a row, getting 22 points (10-14 FGs) in 29 minutes...started all 82 games...had 39 points, his highest-scoring game since he was in high school, in Game 3 of the Western Conference Finals at Seattle, hitting 16-25 FGs...signed a multi-year contract extension with the club on August 20, 1987...in 1987-88 James outlasted a year-long battle with patellar tendinitis in his left knee and wound up as MVP of the NBA Finals...saved the best for last, recording his first triple-double as a pro in Game 7 of the Finals, getting 36 points and his career playoff highs of 16 rebounds and 10 assists (tied)...averaged 19.7 points but posted career lows in FG pct. (.531) and rebounds (5.0)...led Lakers in points (28), rebounds (eight) and assists (four) April 5 vs. Seattle for the first time in his career...scored his regular-season career-high 38 points Feb. 19 at Atlanta as Lakers rallied from a 15-point, fourth-quarter deficit to win in OT...hit career-high .797 FTs, making 32 in a row at one point, but fell below .800 after making 19-28 (.679) in April...finished the season second on the club in scoring for the third year in a row...bothered throughout the season by patellar tendinitis in his left knee which caused him to sit out seven games, five early in the season and two late...had his career-high 10 assists Nov. 15 vs. San Antonio...averaged career highs of 20.5 points and 6.0 rebounds in 1988-89, finishing second on the club in scoring during the regular season for the fourth year in a row...his scoring average then increased in the playoffs for the fifth time in six years, as he averaged another career high of 24.8 points, along with 6.7 rebounds and .567 FGs...recorded his Laker high 40 points in the fourth and final game of the NBA Finals...had playoff highs of 12 rebounds in Game 3 at Phoenix and six assists in Game 4 at Phoenix...James' .555 career FG pct. ranks 9th on the NBA's all-time list, fifth among active players...among all-time Laker records, James ranks third in offensive (1,235) and defensive (2,384) rebounds, fourth in FG pct.(.555) and blocked shots (522), sixth in FGs (4,862), steals (724), and points (11,542), seventh in minutes (20,929), eighth in games (632), and ninth in scoring average (18.3), assists (1,832) and FGA (8,762)...ranks fourth on the NBA's all-time playoff list with a .566 FG pct....on the Laker's all-time playoff list he's fifth in points (2,574), sixth in games (120), and seventh in assists (380) and rebounds (657).

COLLEGE: James passed up his senior year at North Carolina after leading the Tar Heels to a 63-62 win over Georgetown for the NCAA Championship in April, 1982...MVP of the Final Four after scoring a game-high 28 points (13-17 FGs) in the title game...averaged 15.6 points as a junior and his career averages were 14.5 points and 7.2 rebounds with a .541 FG pct....shot .587, .500, and .573 in his three collegiate seasons...named to virtually every All-America team after his junior campaign...second-leading vote-getter (behind Ralph Sampson) on the NBA coaches' All-America team that year and shared College Player of the Year honors bestowed by the First Interstate Bank Athletic Foundation with his ACC rival from Virginia...the Tar Heels were 71-13 (.845) during his three years there...missed the final 14 games of his freshman campaign due to a broken ankle...All-ACC as a sophomore and a junior...also named to the All-ACC Tournament team both years and Tournament MVP as a junior.

PERSONAL: James was a unanimous prep All-America at Ashbrook High, where he averaged 21.5 points and 12.5 rebounds as a senior...lived up to a commitment he made when he left North Carolina early by returning to school to earn his degree...while in college he would work during the summers with the aged and mentally retarded...James' wife, Angela gave birth to their first child last March, a baby girl named Sable Alexandria...Angela is a former North Carolina cheer-leader, and an aspiring model and actress, who appeared in the TV movie, "Hollywood Detective"...Angela was one of the songwriters on the Lakers' "Just Say No" anti-drug rap song, which was recorded and put into video form in the summer of 1987...the Worthys live in Los Angeles with their two dogs, Bossy and Hammer, and their two cats, Missy and Baxter, and will be moving to a new home in the Pacific Palisades sometime during the season.

JAMES'S TOP CAREER PERFORMANCES

SCORING		REBOUNDS	
1. 38 @ Atlanta (2-19-88)		1. 17 @ Utah (11-28-84)	
2. 38 vs Sacramento (4-20-89)		2. 16 @ Seattle (12-13-84)	
3. 37 @ Portland (4-8-84)		3. 15 vs LA Clippers (1-18-89)	
4. 37 @ Denver (12-13-85)		4. 14 vs Golden State (12-23-83)	
5. 35 vs Boston (2-16-86)		5. 14 vs Portland (11-4-84)	
6. 34 vs Golden State (3-20-86)		6. 14 vs Phoenix (12-21-84)	
7. 33 @ Chicago (12-1-86)		7. 14 vs Houston (4-10-86)	
8. 33 @ Chicago (1-20-86)		8. 14 vs New York (1-24-89)	
9. 33 @ Denver (11-15-88)			
10. 33 vs Detroit (2-14-89)			

NBA REGULAR SEASON

SEASON	TEAM	G	MIN	FGM-FGA	PCT	3-PT	FTM-FTA	PCT	OFF	DEF	TOT	AST	PF-DQ	ST	TO	BS	PTS	AVG
1982-83	LA	77	1970	447-772	.579	1-4	138-221	.624	157	242	399	132	221-2	91	178	64	1033	13.4
1983-84	LA	82	2415	495-890	.556	0-6	195-257	.759	157	358	515	207	244-5	77	181	70	1185	14.5
1984-85	LA	80	2696	610-1066	.572	0-7	190-245	.776	169	342	511	201	196-0	87	198	67	1410	17.6
1985-86	LA	75	2454	629-1086	.579	0-13	242-314	.771	136	251	387	201	195-0	82	149	77	1500	20.0
1986-87	LA	82	2819	651-1207	.539	0-13	292-389	.751	158	308	466	226	206-0	108	168	83	1594	19.4
1987-88	LA	75	2655	617-1161	.531	2-16	242-304	.796	129	245	374	289	175-1	72	155	55	1478	19.7
1988-89	LA	81	2960	702-1282	.548	2-23	251-321	.782	169	320	489	288	175-0	108	182	56	1657	20.5
1989-90	LA	80	2960	711-1298	.548	15-49	248-317	.782	160	318	478	288	190-0	99	160	49	1685	21.1
Totals		632	20929	4862-8762	.555	20-131	1798-2368	.759	1235	2384	3619	1832	1602-8	724	1371	521	11542	18.3

PLAYOFFS

SEASON	TEAM	G	MIN	FGM-FGA	PCT	3-PT	FTM-FTA	PCT	OFF	DEF	TOT	AST	PF-DQ	ST	TO	BS	PTS	AVG
1983-84	LA	21	708	164-274	.599	1-2	42-69	.609	36	69	105	56	57-0	27	39	11	371	17.7
1984-85	LA	19	626	166-267	.622	1-2	75-111	.676	35	61	96	41	53-1	17	26	13	408	21.5
1985-86	LA	14	539	121-217	.558	0-4	32-47	.681	22	43	65	45	43-0	16	36	10	274	19.6
1986-87	LA	18	681	176-298	.591	0-2	73-97	.753	31	70	101	63	42-1	28	40	22	425	23.6
1987-88	LA	24	896	204-390	.523	1-9	97-128	.758	53	86	139	106	58-0	33	55	19	506	21.1
1988-89	LA	15	600	153-270	.567	3-8	63-80	.788	37	64	101	42	36-0	18	33	16	372	24.8
1989-90	LA	9	366	90-171	.526	2-8	36-43	.837	11	39	50	27	18-0	14	22	3	318	24.2
Totals		120	4416	1074-1887	.569	8-35	418-575	.727	225	432	657	380	256-2	153	251	94	2574	21.5

ELDEN CAMPBELL   #41

Hight: 6-11
Weight: 215
Position: Forward
Born: July 23, 1968
High School: Morningside (Inglewood)
College: Clemson '90
Residence: Inglewood

Selected by the Lakers in the first round of the 1990 college draft (27th overall).

COLLEGE: Elden was the Lakers' first round selection in the 1990 college draft...finished his college career as the all-time leading scorer in Clemson history with 1,880 points...averaged 16.4 points and career-high 8.0 rebounds per game to lead Clemson to their first conference championship and the East Regional Semifinals as a senior...named to All-ACC first team, leading conference in blocked shots with 97 and ranking seventh in field goal percentage (.522) and steals (54)...was also an honorable mention All-America as a senior...finished as fourth leading rebounder in school history with 836...his 334 career blocks are fifth-highest total in ACC history, and second behind Tree Rollins in Clemson history...Joined Rollins as only players in school history to exceed 1,000 points, 500 rebounds and 200 blocked shots in a career...a key reserve his freshman year, Elden started three of 31 games, averaging 8.8 points and 4.1 rebounds per game...shot career-high .702 (59-84) from free throw line and led the Tigers in blocked shots with 62...selected to All-ACC third team as a sophomore, starting 27 games and ranking 10th in the nation with .629 field goal percentage...averaged career-high 18.8 ppg, and led ACC in blocked shots for first of three consecutive seasons with 88...named to All-ACC second team following junior season, when he ranked ninth in the nation in blocked shots with 87 (3.0)...averaged 17.5 points and 7.7 rebounds per game.

PERSONAL: Nicknamed "Big E" by teammates, Elden was one member of Clemson's "Duo of Doom"...the other member was his roommate Dale Davis...Elden was invited to the 1988 Olympic tryouts in Colorado Springs, survived several Olympic Trial cuts (to final 27), then went with coach George Raveling's U.S. Select team to Europe...also went to Moscow as a member of the Nike NIT All-Stars that same summer, being the leading scorer (17.0) and second leading rebounder (7.0)...Clemson was the only ACC team to recruit Campbell...Kansas, UCLA, USC, and Pepperdine were his other options, but he wanted to play in the ACC...Elden attended Morningside High School in Inglewood where he earned All-City recognition.

SAM PERKINS

14

Height: 6-9 1/2
Weight: 250
Position: Forward/Center
Born: June 14, 1961 (New York, N.Y.)
High School: Shaker Heights (Latham, N.Y.)
College: North Carolina '84
Residence:

Signed by the Lakers as a free agent on August 6, 1990.

1989-90: As a restricted free agent, Sam was a brief training camp holdout last season, as he evaluated his long-term options...eventually elected to re-sign with the Mavericks, inking a one-year contract on October 12...averaged a career-high 15.9 points in 76 outings with Dallas, surpassing the 15.4 mark he posted in 1985-86, his second year as a pro...started final 70 appearances after initially beginning the campaign as Dallas' sixth-man...scored in double figures 67 times, 20 or more points on 17 occasions, 30 or more twice, and exceeded the 40 point plateau once...led the Mavericks in scoring 11 times, rebounding on 16 occasions...scored a career-high 45 points against the Warriors at Golden State on April 12, topping his previous high of 32 points also established vs. Golden State in 1986...his 45 point performance, the fifth highest in Dallas history, included 30 first half points, 22 in the opening quarter...was the Mavericks' third-best shooter, amassing a .493 field goal percentage, second only to the .503 he registered in 1985-86...surpassed Mark Aguirre as the Mavericks' all-time leading rebounder at Washington on December 12...averaged 7.5 rebounds in 35.1 minutes of action...dished out a career-high 175 assists, leading the Dallas frontcourt in that category...although utilized primarily as a power forward early in the season, Adrian Dantley's season-ending leg injury necessitated his move to small forward for the Mavericks' final 32 games...averaged 15.0 points and 7.3 rebounds vs. Portland as the Mavericks were quickly eliminated from playoff competition in the first round...as a six year NBA veteran, became an unrestricted free-agent at seasons end.

CAREER: Sam was a first-round draft choice of the Dallas Mavericks in 1984, the fourth player selected overall...Dallas acquired the pick from Cleveland four years prior in exchange for Mike Bratz...throughout his six seasons as a Maverick, he exemplified versatility, starting at both forward positions as well as center...averaged between 14.2 and 15.9 points each of his last five seasons...appeared in each of the Mavericks' 82 games for the lone time in his career as a rookie in 1984-85, averaging a career-low 11.0 points...named to the NBA's All-Rookie Team that year...averaged a career playoff high his initial season, scoring at an 18.8 clip in four post-season contests...recorded the only 30 point/20 rebound performance in Mavericks history during his second campaign (1985-86), scoring 31 points and grabbing 20 rebounds at Houston on December 12, 1986...the 20 rebounds signifies a career-high, as does the 94 blocked shots he totaled that same season...promoted to a permanent starting position for the 1986-87 campaign, appearing as such in each of his 80 games played...averaged 14.8 points and 7.7 rebounds as a full-time starter, leading Dallas to the Midwest Division Championship for the lone time in club history...averaged 14.2 points and 8.0 rebounds in 75 outings, each as a starter, for the Mavericks in 1987-88...sank 80-of-83 free throws to conclude the regular season, including 33 straight at one point...contributed 13.5 points and 6.6 rebounds in 17 playoff games that season as the upstart Mavericks forced the Lakers to a seventh game in the Western Conference Finals...became the first Maverick in franchise history to collect 600-plus rebounds for five consecutive seasons when he averaged

a career-high 8.8 boards during the 1988-89 campaign...led the Mavericks in rebounding, both offensive (235) and defensive (453), in 1988-89...posted career-highs also in average minutes played and free throw percentage, 36.7 and .833, respectively...his five blocked shots vs. Charlotte on November 17, 1988 represents a career-high...concluded his six-year stint with the Mavericks having established himself among the club's all-time leaders in several categories: first in total rebounds (3,767), second in offensive rebounds (1,226), second in defensive rebounds (2,541), third in blocked shots (444), fifth in assists (854), fifth in scoring (6,766), and fifth in games played (471).

COLLEGE: Averaged 17.6 points per game and 9.6 rebounds as a senior, 15.9 points per game and 8.6 boards for his career...UNC's third three-time all-America following Phil Ford (1976-78) and Jack Cobb (1924-26)...won Lapchick Award as nation's outstanding senior...ACC rookie of the year in 1980-81 when the Tar Heels lost to Indiana in the NCAA finals...as a sophomore Perkins averaged 14.3 points and 7.8 rebounds while playing center for the NCAA champs...high game of college career was 36 points vs. Ralph Sampson and Virginia 1/15/83.

PERSONAL: Sam co-captained the 1984 gold medal-winning U.S. Olympic team...that followed titles in the 1983 Pan Am Games, the 1982 NCAA tourney and a national high school all-star tournament in 1980...says former UNC teammate James Worthy has been his biggest basketball influence...owns a pet keeshond, Sasha...grew up in Brooklyn...moved to Latham, N.Y., an Albany suburb to continue his education...earned his degree in Communications at UNC...lefthanded...single...given name is Samuel Bruce Perkins.

TONY SMITH

Height: 6-4
Weight: 195
Position: Guard
Born: June 14, 1968 (Wauwatosa, WI)
High School: Wauwatosa East '86
College: Marquette University '90

Selected by the Lakers in the second round of the 1990 NBA draft (51st overall).

COLLEGE: Tony holds Marquette University's single-season scoring records of 689 points and a 23.8 scoring average in 1989-90...the 6-4 guard, named to the first team All-Midwestern Collegiate Conference, ended his career as MU's third all-time leading scorer with 1,688 points...he was also named to the All-Midwest second team and honorable mention All-American selection by Basketball Weekly, and honorable mention by both the Associated Press and The Sporting News...earned four MU team awards last year including MVP...shot .520 from the field and .429 from three-point range in his four seasons, averaging 14.9 points and 4.2 rebounds...finished second on Marquette's all-time assists (469) and steals (190) charts...was third overall in MCC last season in assists (5.8) and FT percentage (.865)...averaged 27.2 points over his last 10 games with six games of 30-plus points...averaged 8.1 points his freshman season and 13.1 points as a sophomore and was named MU's Most Improved Player following the 1987-88 season.

PERSONAL: Tony was an All-State player at Wauwatosa East High School in Wisconsin...as a senior, he led the Red Raiders to a 24-1 record and an 18-0 record in the North Shore Conference...averaged 21 points and 8 rebounds his senior year...was named North Shore Conference Player of the Year by the Milwaukee Sentinel...an outstanding athlete, Tony was a two-time state triple jump champion in Class A track...he ran the 110 meter hurdles in 14.5 seconds, high jumped 6-6, long jumped 22-6 and also played varsity volleyball for the Red Raiders...Tony participated in the Southern California Summer Pro League this summer, where he averaged 12.7 points, 6.6 rebounds and 2.9 rebounds in 10 games, shooting .560 FGs and .850 FTs.

TERRY TEAGLE   #20

Height: 6-5
Weight: 195
Position: Guard/Forward
Born: April 10, 1960 (Broaddus, Texas)
High School: Broaddus
College: Baylor, 1982

Acquired by the Lakers on September 25, 1990 from Golden State for 1991 first round draft choice.

1989-90: Terry averaged career highs of 16.1 points, 4.5 rebounds and 29.0 minutes for the Warriors last season...saw action in all 82 games for the first time in three seasons and finished the season with the team's longest active streak of regular season games played (134)...Warriors were 9-0 when he scored 26 or more points...was named NBA Player of the Week for the first time in his eight-year career on Jan. 8 after averaging 33.0 ppg (.585 FG, .920 FT) and 7.0 rebounds while leading the Warriors to three straight victories...scored a career-high 44 points by making 16-26 FGs, including 12 straight in the first half, and 12-of-12 tried from the free throw line vs. Utah Jan. 2...Equalled his previous career high with 36 points in the first half...Took a Chris Mullin pass and scored the game-winning basket with one-tenth of a second remaining vs. Milwaukee Dec. 2...the win snapped a 12-game losing streak against the Bucks and gave Don Nelson his first-ever win against his former team...season highlights included making two free throws with 7.8 seconds remaining in a 133-131 win vs. the Lakers on Jan. 6...reached double-figures in scoring 65 times, 20 or more points 24 times, 30 or more points five times, and 40 or more points once...led the team in scoring nine times, paced them in rebounding eleven times and had two double-doubles.

CAREER: Terry started 44 games as a rookie with Houston in 1982-83...saw his playing time drop from 23.4 minutes per game to 9.1 minutes in his second season...was released by Houston on Oct. 23, 1984...signed with Detroit on Nov. 7, 1984 and totaled two points and five minutes in two games before being waived on Nov. 20, 1984...moved across town to join the Detroit Spirits of the CBA where he averaged 19.5 points in 40 games before signing with the Warriors...appeared in all 19 of the team's remaining games in 1984-85 and started the final three contests...played in all 82 games in each of the following two seasons and was named CBA in the NBA Player of the Year for 1985-86...posted his career-high of 12 rebounds vs. the Clippers on Jan. 16, 1987...DNP-CD in 16 contests, including 13 straight in Dec....averaged 17.5 points on .485 FGs in 41 games as a starter.

COLLEGE: Finished his career at Baylor as the all-time scoring leader in Southwest Conference history with 2,189 points...was a three-time All-SWC First Team selection and was named Second Team All-American as a senior...led the Bears in scoring and rebounding in each of his last three seasons...led the conference in scoring as a sophomore, then finished third as a junior and second as a senior.

PERSONAL: Terry's hometown of Broaddus, Texas is on the northern edge of the Sam Rayburn Reservoir, approximately 60 miles north of Beaumont...the farm community of about 200 people may be the smallest hometown of any current NBA player...some of the locals have put up satellite TV dishes, primarily to watch him play...he and his wife Debra have one daughter, Mikala...Terry spends his summers in suburban Houston, where he enjoys being with his family and swimming...Number one professional goal is to win a world championship.

JERRY BUSS

Jerry Buss purchased the Los Angeles Lakers, the Los Angeles Kings of the National Hockey League, The Forum and a 13,000-acre Kern County ranch in June, 1979, for $67.5 million in what was then the largest sports transaction of all time.

In the 11 seasons of his ownership, a modern sports dynasty of no small proportions evolved. These Laker teams have won five world championships and reached the world-championship round eight times. They have won 72 percent of their games, 26 of 32 playoff series and have averaged 70 wins a season, including playoffs.

A graduate of the University of Wyoming with a Bachelor's degree, Buss took his Ph.D. in Chemistry from the University of Southern California. After a brief career in the aerospace industry, Buss and Frank Mariani, an aerospace engineer, used their scientific training and facility with mathematics to launch a career in real estate. They parlayed an original $1,000 investment in a West Los Angeles apartment building into what became a multi-hundred-million-dollar real estate business at its height.

However, since his emergence into major league sports, Buss has reduced his involvement in real estate and has increased his activity in sports. He has initiated many innovative changes in the marketing of the Lakers and other events at The Forum, including a major advertising agreement with Great Western Bank that has resulted in the facility being renamed The Great Western Forum.

In 1985 Buss and Bill Daniels launched Prime Ticket Network, now one of the premier regional sports cable television networks.

Buss' two daughters are actively involved in his sports enterprises. Jeanie heads the tennis and volleyball operations and Janie is director of special events.

Buss' blue-jean lifestyle is as casual as his business operations are mathematically precise. He jumps into both with great enthusiasm, as he does his involvement in community work. Buss devotes a large measure of his time and resources to many community-serving causes. He is most diligent in his support of education and of the disadvantaged young and elderly.

JERRY WEST

In Jerry West's eight years as the Laker's General Manager, the club has won three NBA titles while averaging better than 60 wins per season. But success within the marriage of Jerry West and the Lakers should be nothing new: since the club moved to Los Angeles in 1960 it has participated in the playoffs in all but two seasons —and those were the only two seasons (1974-75 and 1975-76) in which he was not affiliated with the club.

Jerry is better-known as one of the greatest players in NBA history after a 14-year Laker career. When he retired after the 1973-74 campaign he had scored 25,192 points, the third player to reach the 25,000 mark, and still the sixth-highest total in NBA history. His 27.0 scoring average is the fourth-highest in NBA history and he ranks among the all-time leaders in several other categories.

Jerry was the all-time NBA playoff leader in points (4,457) and assists (970) until Kareem Abdul-Jabbar and Earvin Johnson, respectively, passed him in 1985 post-season play. His 29.1 scoring average in the playoffs is still among the highest in NBA history and he remains the Lakers' all-time scoring leader.

Among his most memorable accomplishments were compiling a 40.6 scoring average during the 1965 playoffs and sinking a 60-foot shot to send Game 3 of the 1970 Championship Series against the New York Knicks into overtime.

Jerry was selected to the All-NBA first team 10 times, the second team twice, the All-Defensive first team four times and second team once. He was selected to play in the All-Star Game for 13 consecutive seasons and was MVP of the 1972 classic at The Forum, and NBA Playoff MVP in 1969 despite playing for the losing team.

He averaged 25.8 points for the 1971-72 Lakers, which set NBA records by winning 33 straight games and finishing 69-13 before bringing the first NBA title to Los Angeles. Jerry was elected to the Basketball Hall of Fame in 1979 and was named to the NBA's 35th Anniversary team in 1980.

Jerry retired prior to the 1974-75 season and returned to the Lakers for the 1976-77 season, replacing Bill Sharman as the club's head coach. He posted a 145-101 record and his clubs reached the playoffs in each of his three seasons at the helm. His first club finished with a 53-29 record, the best in the NBA that season, and he led the club into the playoffs after the two-year absence.

Following the 1978-79 campaign Jerry served the Lakers for three years as a special consultant, with the primary responsibility of scouting college players. Prior to the 1982-83 season he was elevated to his present position as the club's General Manager, where he oversees the day-to-day operation of the club and all player personnel decisions.

Jerry attended West Virginia University, where he set 12 school records, graduated with a 24.8 scoring average and was a two-time All-America before becoming the Lakers' first pick in the 1960 college draft.

Before entering the NBA Jerry served as co-captain of the gold-medal winning U.S. Olympic basketball team in Rome in 1960, a squad generally touted as the greatest in Olympic history. He was also a member of the victorious U.S. squad in the 1958 Pan American Games.

Jerry was born on May 28, 1938 in Chelyan, West Virginia, and first drew national attention as a high school star. As a senior at East Bank High School he led his team to the state title and became the first player in the state's history to score over 900 points in a season, averaging 32.2 points a game.

Jerry and his wife, Karen, reside in Bel Air with their sons, Ryan and Jonathan. Jerry has three other sons, David, Mark and Michael. from a previous marriage.

MITCHELL KUPCHAK

Mitch Kupchak assumed even greater responsibility last season in his fourth year as the Lakers' assistant general manager.

Among the areas that Mitch oversees are the club's pre-season schedule, Summer League team and training camp in Hawaii. He also assists in the club's scouting of college players and continues to update the basketball staff's computer system, while working with Jerry West in the day-to-day management of the club.

Mitch was a first-round draft choice of the Washington Bullets in 1976 and spent his first five seasons there. He was a major contributor off the bench to the Bullets' NBA Championship club in 1978, and remains one of 15 players in NBA history to have played on Championship clubs with two different franchises.

In August, 1981, he was acquired by the Lakers in exchange for Jim Chones, Brad Holland and two draft picks. Mitch was a starter for the Lakers for the first 26 games of the 1981-82 campaign, averaging 14.3 points and 8.1 rebounds, before suffering multiple injuries to his left knee which required two surgeries. It was feared, even expected, that he would never play again, but Mitch proved the doctors wrong by returning to the Lakers in November, 1983 after undergoing daily therapy for 16 months.

He was a major contributor off the bench as the club captured the 1985 title, but suffered a series of injuries the following year, including a contusion to his larynx which made him virtually inaudible for several months, a sprained ankle, and two sprains of his previously injured left knee.

Prior to the start of the 1986-87 campaign, after another lengthy rehabilitation following arthroscopic knee surgery, Mitch accepted an offer to assume his present position and announced his retirement from playing.

When Mitch signed to play with the Lakers in the summer of 1981, one of the provisions in his long-term contract was that he would continue to work for Laker owner Dr. Jerry Buss in some capacity following his retirement from playing. In preparation for that career move, he studied for an MBA degree at UCLA during his spare time, and received that degree in February, 1987.

Mitch was born in Hicksville, New York on May 24, 1954 and starred at Brentwood High School on Long Island. He was a standout at the University of North Carolina, named an "All-American" in 1976, and then was named the league's Player of the Year as a senior. He was the starting center of the gold-medal winning U.S. team in the 1976 Olympics, and was also a member of the gold-medal winning U.S. team in the 1973 World University games.

Mitch is single and resides in Brentwood.

BILL SHARMAN

The Lakers are extremely pleased to have basketball legend Bill Sharman returning this season to the Laker front office in his capacity as special consultant for the club.

Serving as the Laker's president from 1982 to 1988, Bill retired after the Lakers' 1988 NBA title rewarded him with his 12th pro basketball championship ring. The 12 championships were spread over four teams in three leagues from four different perspectives.

His first four championships came while he was playing with the Boston Celtics (1957, 1959, 1960 and 1961) during a career which eventually saw him named to the NBA's 10-man Silver Anniversary Team in 1970 and later inducted into the Basketball Hall of Fame in 1974.

His fifth title came in 1962, when he assumed the head coaching position with the Cleveland Pipers in mid-season and led the club to the American Basketball League crown. Nine years later, he coached the Utah Stars to an American Basketball Association title.

Bill has been a part of all six NBA titles the Lakers have captured since moving to Los Angeles in the early "60s. After leading the Stars to the ABA title in 1970-71, Bill coached the record-setting, 69-13 Lakers the following year, guiding that team to an NBA-record 33 consecutive victories. He served as the club's general manager when it annexed NBA titles in 1980 and 1982, and was the club president for its most recent championships in 1985, 1987, and 1988.

The Washington Capitals drafted Bill in the second round in 1950 and he played in 31 games during his rookie season. He was selected by Fort Wayne in the 1951 dispersal draft, but was later traded to the Celtics.

In addition to the four titles, the Celtics finished in first place five times and never suffered a losing season during his 10 campaigns there. He was named to the All-NBA team seven times and participated in eight All-Star Games, earning MVP honors in the 1955 contest and sinking a legendary 88-foot shot in the 1958 game.

Arguably the greatest shooter during the NBA's first generation, Bill was the first guard to shoot .400 from the floor for a season and his .884 free throw percentage remains among the highest in league history. He averaged 17.8 points in 711 regular-season games and improved his performance in 78 playoff appearances by averaging 18.5 points and hitting 91 percent of his free throws.

After retiring from the Celtics in 1961, Bill began a distinguished coaching career and he remains the only person to have coached championship teams in three different pro leagues. He began as coach of the Los Angeles Jets of the ABL in 1961-62 but took command of the Pipers after the Jets disbanded in mid-season.

In his seven seasons as NBA head coach, which began with the San Francisco Warriors from 1966-68, his teams won four divisional titles and wound up with a 330-240 (.581) record. Bill's four Laker clubs won better than 60 percent of their games.

Bill moved into the Lakers' front office following the 1975-76 season, first as General Manager and, following the team's 1982 Championship season, as President. He was responsible for several transactions that have maintained the club's level of excellence, including the trade that provided the club with the No. 1 pick of James Worthy.

Bill and his wife, Joyce, live in Marina del Rey. He has two daughters, Nancy and Janice, and two sons, Tom and Jerry, from a previous marriage.

MICHAEL DUNLEAVY

Mike Dunleavy takes over in 1990 as head coach of the Los Angeles Lakers, the recognized team of the '80s. He is 36 years old and he has never been a head coach in the NBA before.

But the Lakers are used to this. In 1981, the Lakers hired a 36-year-old former player who had no previous NBA head coaching experience. A fellow by the name of Pat Riley.

And that worked out pretty well.

"When you look to replace someone like Pat Riley, the choices are difficult," General Manager Jerry West said June 11, 1990, the day he named Mike as head coach. "Mike may have been a sixth-round pick as a player, but as a coach he's our No. 1 pick."

After grooming for the past three seasons as an assistant coach with the Milwaukee Bucks, Mike takes over a team that posted the best regular-season record in the NBA at 63-19. He plans to emphasize a disciplined defense and a balanced offense that removes some of the daily scoring burden from Magic Johnson and James Worthy.

"Not many changes of personnel are needed to stay competitive," Mike said. "I happen to think this is a terrific team. There is a lot of talent and character, and I'm looking forward to anticipating an NBA Finals. I want a ring on my finger."

As a head coach, Mike can draw upon a fine playing career, one that as of last season still had not ended. As a player, he was known for floor burns and jump shots, and that hustle and precision are qualities that he still exudes on and off the court.

Mike averaged double-figure scoring in each of his four seasons at the University of South Carolina. In 1976, he was drafted in the sixth round (99th overall) by the Philadelphia 76ers, for whom he played for parts of two seasons.

In 1977, Mike served as player-coach of the Carolina Lightning in the short-lived All-American Basketball Alliance. He finished the 1977-78 NBA season in Houston and remained with the club through the 1981-82 season.

After a year with San Antonio, he left for New York, working for Merrill Lynch on Wall Street.

"I really enjoyed working on Wall Street," Mike said. "It was a lot of fun and I learned a lot. But to me, the difference between basketball and Wall Street is that was work. I really *enjoy* basketball. I put in long hours, probably more than on Wall Street."

He returned to the NBA the following season when an injury-depleted Milwaukee Bucks team came calling. In the final 17 regular-season games and 15 playoff games, he averaged a career-high 11.2 points.

Nineteen games into the 1984-85 season, Mike suffered a serious back injury when an airplane jerked suddenly while taxiing. That brought him into coaching, and in 1987 he joined the Bucks as a bench assistant.

"I really try and get involved in just about every facet of the game," Mike said. "Maybe because of my age and my athletic ability, I can still play and work with the players on an individual basis. That's a lot of fun for me to still be able to do that."

For the past two seasons in Milwaukee, he played and worked with the players in more than practice. Whenever the injury bug bit the Bucks particularly hard, the club simply signed Mike to a series of 10-day contracts: He played in two games in 1988-89 and five last season.

But the Lakers hired Mike first and foremost as a head coach. It's a position he feels well prepared for, thanks to an apprenticeship under Milwaukee's Del Harris.

"I couldn't have asked for a better environment for on-the-job training," he said. "I feel very comfortable with X's and O's. Del gave me great responsibility. He allows his assistants to have a lot of input and does not try to stifle their creativity."

Mike was born on March 21, 1954 in Brooklyn, N.Y. and attended Nazareth High School there. He and his wife, Emily, have three sons, Michael, William Baker, and James.

BILL BERTKA

The Lakers' veteran assistant coach has pretty much "seen it all" in his 40-plus years as a player, coach and administrator.

Bill played his college ball at Kent State University and played in the old National Industrial Basketball League before embarking on careers in coaching and scouting.

He served as head coach at Hancock College in Santa Maria from 1954-57, leading the team to a 42-game winning streak, a 97-13 overall record and a Junior College State Championship in 1957. He then left Hancock and returned to his alma mater, where he served as head coach for four years and helped elevate Kent State's program to the major-college level.

Bill, 63, is actually in his second tour of duty with the Lakers. He originally joined the club in 1968, serving as the club's chief scout and director of player personnel for six years. He then joined the New Orleans Jazz when the club was formed in 1974 and served that club in a variety of roles, including general manager, director of player personnel and assistant coach, and was the primary architect for the franchise during the first eight years of the team's existence, before rejoining the Lakers early in the 1981-82 campaign.

Bill's duties range from compiling and organizing scouting reports and statistical data, to keeping tabs on prospects both in college, the CBA and Europe, and working one-on-one before and after practices with a developing player.

He is perhaps best known as the founder of Bertka Views, the most successful college scouting service in the country, now operated by his wife, Solveig. Many of the nation's premier college basketball programs utilize Bertka Views as their sole scouting service. Meanwhile, Bill, long recognized for his scouting ability, maintains access to more scouting reports on college talent than anyone.

Bill had the double distinction in 1989 of being inducted into a Hall of Fame in each of his hometowns. In May, he was inducted into the Santa Barbara Sports Hall of Fame, where he makes his present home. In October, he was inducted into the Summit County (Ohio) Sports Hall of Fame, where he grew up.

Bill and Solveig have two daughters, Britt and Kris, and make their home in Santa Barbara.

RANDY PFUND

Generally regarded as one of the best young assistant coaches in the NBA, Randy has come a long way from the 33-year-old assistant at an NAIA school who joined the Laker staff five years ago.

Randy was working as a high school teacher and coach in Illinois for two years before he quit and took a gamble in an attempt to get a college coaching position. Randy talked his way into a job as an unpaid voluntary assistant at Westmont College in Santa Barbara, where he remained for eight years. Eventually, he began to get paid for his efforts, and also took over as director of the school's booster organization.

While at Westmont he became familiar with another Santa Barbara resident involved with coaching, Bill Bertka, and when Dave Wohl resigned as Laker assistant to become head coach of the New Jersey Nets prior to the 1985-86 season, then Laker coach Pat Riley selected Randy as his successor, citing his scouting and administrative experience as major factors in the decision.

Randy has also demonstrated potential as a head coach for the Lakers in the Southern California Summer Pro League, having guided the Lakers to the League title in 1987.

Randy grew up in Wheaton, Illinois, and starred in basketball and football at North High School there. He later earned honorable mention All-American honors in basketball at Wheaton College, where his father, Lee, was head coach.

Randy is single and lives in Marina Del Rey.

JIM EYEN

Jim Eyen, 34, is the newest member of the Laker coaching staff, having signed with the club last September 1.

During the middle of the 1988-89 season, Randy Pfund relinquished his duties as the Lakers' advance scout to concentrate more on working with the club, with the responsibility of scouting upcoming opponents assumed by Ronnie Lester.

Last year, with Lester returning to college scouting, the advance scouting responsibilities fell on Jim Eyen.

Eyen was in his fifth season as an assistant coach at his alma mater, UCSB, when the Los Angeles Clippers asked him to join their bench on January 23, 1989. Prior to returning to UCSB, he served as coach at Dos Pueblos High School for two years (1982-84), and as an assistant at Santa Barbara City College for three seasons (1979-82).

Jim played high school basketball and baseball and played freshman basketball at UCSB before opting to play semi-pro baseball. He received his B.A. in Communication Studies from UCSB in 1980, and an M.A. in education from Azusa Pacific in 1984.

Jim continues the pipeline from Santa Barbara to the Laker bench, joining fellow assistants Bill Bertka and Randy Pfund with Santa Barbara connections. Bertka has lived in Santa Barbara for years, while Pfund joined the Lakers after spending eight years as an assistant at Westmont College there.

Jim is single and resides in Playa Del Rey.

GARY VITTI

Gary Vitti, who enters his seventh season as the club's trainer, monitors the club throughout the year, not just the season, using state-of-the-art methods in conditioning, dieting, stretching and testing.

While the 35-year-old is responsible for the care, prevention and treatment of injuries to Laker players, his responsibilities don't end there. Among his other duties are overissuing the club's transportation and accommodations on the road as well as arranging the team's practice schedule.

Gary grew up in Stamford, Connecticut and attended Stamford Catholic High School. He earned a B.S. form Southern Connnecticut State in 1976 and an M.S. in sports medicine from the University of Utah in 1982.

In addition to studying at the University of Utah he spent two years as a trainer there as well as two years as an assistant trainer with the Utah Jazz. He then served as the head athletic trainer at the University of Portland for two years before joining the Lakers prior to the 1984-85 season, and has been a valuable cog on three NBA Championship clubs since then.

Gary is frequently asked to speak about conditioning to various groups, has supervised physiological profile studies published in English and Japanese and has written a monthly column for <u>Sports Medicine Digest.</u>

Gary, his wife Chris, and their daughter, Rachel, live in Manhattan Beach.

CHICK HEARN

Chick Hearn, the only play-by-play man the club has had since moving to Los Angeles, enters his 31st season providing his colorful "words-eye-view." But don't plan any Farewell Tours just yet. Chick enters this season with a string of 2,336 consecutive broadcasts (regular-season and playoffs) and last missed a Laker game in November 1965.

The Lakers moved to Los Angeles prior to the 1960-61 season, and did not broadcast games on radio that year until the playoffs. Chick was behind the microphone for that first post-season broadcast, and he's been there ever since.

Born Francis Dayle Hearn, Chick grew up in Aurora, Illinois and attended Bradley University. He was given the nickname "Chick" when, as an AAU basketball player, he was handed a box of sneakers only to be surprised to find a chicken inside.

Chick came to Los Angeles in 1956 to broadcast USC football and basketball and later did a nightly radio sports show that earned him two Emmy Awards in the 1960s. He joined the Lakers shortly thereafter and has remained to describe the action of six NBA Championship clubs. Although best-known for his work with the Lakers, Chick has broadcast an assortment of sporting events, including NCAA football, UNLV basketball, PGA golf tournaments, the first Ali-Frazier fight, the Rose Bowl, the East-West Shrine football game, celebrity tennis and Bowling for Dollars. He has broadcast as many as three Laker and three UNLV games in a single week. In addition to Laker radio/tv simulcasts Chick also broadcasts Forum boxing and tennis events and Summer League basketball on the Prime Ticket Network.

Chick's near-non-stop work schedule also includes numerous commercials and movie spots and he's a popular after-dinner speaker. Four years ago he recorded a hit rap record, "Wrap Around", and he also helped create "Chick's Dream Game" fantasy tapes. He has received a Golden Mike Award, has twice been named National Sportscaster of the Year and has been feted by numerous other groups, including the Anti-Defamation League.

Among Chick's other career highlights are "Chick Hearn Night", which the team held in his honor on March 28, 1981 and included a congratulatory telegram from another former midwestern sportscaster, President Reagan, and the rainy day in the fall of 1986, when a star bearing his name was installed on Hollywood Boulevard's "Walk of Fame."

Chick and his wife, Marge, live in Encino.

STU LANTZ

It is easy to understand if Stu Lantz relates to Bud Abbott. The difference is, instead of feeding straight lines to Lou Costello, Lantz has Chick Hearn as a partner.

Stu begins his fourth year as commentator alongside Hearn, and his insight has been a valuable part of Laker broadcasts.

Of course, Stu and the Lakers are not a new partnership, either, as he played in 109 regular-season games and averaged 7.1 points for the Lakers between 1974-77.

Stu graduated from the University of Nebraska in 1968 and was a third-round draft choice of the San Diego Rockets. He spent his first three seasons in San Diego and enjoyed his best pro campaign in 1970-71, his third season, when he averaged 20.6 points per game for the Rockets.

He also played for the Houston Rockets, Detroit Pistons and New Orleans Jazz before being traded in December 1974 to the Lakers, where he remained through the 1976-77 campaign. He sat out that entire final season due to a back injury before retiring.

Following his premature retirement, hastened by a back injury, Stu immediately embarked on a broadcasting career. He served as a commentator for the San Diego Clippers, San Diego State University, the University of Nevada-Las Vegas and CBS, and prior to working Laker games broadcast Summer League action with Chick Hearn on the Prime Ticket Network.

In addition to his duties with the Lakers Stu is vice president of Micro Electronic Components, Inc. in Carlsbad, and stays close to the game in the summer by assisting in the operation of the renowned Newell Big-Man Camp, as well as a shooting camp in the San Diego area. Stu and his wife, Linda, live in San Diego with their three children, Todd, Kristin and Shane.

Lakers
Records

ALL-TIME TOP LAKERS PERFORMANCES (GAME)

POINTS

Elgin Baylor	vs New York	11-15-60	71
Wilt Chamberlain	vs Phoenix	02-09-69	66
Elgin Baylor	vs Boston	11-08-59	64
Elgin Baylor	vs Philadelphia	12-02-61	63
Jerry West	vs New York	01-17-62	63
George Mikan	vs Rochester	01-20-52	61
Wilt Chamberlain	vs Cincinnati	01-26-69	60
Elgin Baylor	vs Detroit	02-16-61	57
Elgin Baylor	vs Syracuse	01-24-61	56
Elgin Baylor	vs Cincinnati	02-25-59	55

REBOUNDS

Wilt Chamberlain	vs Boston	03-07-69	42
Wilt Chamberlain	vs Baltimore	03-09-69	38
Wilt Chamberlain	vs San Francisco	02-02-69	35
Wilt Chamberlain	vs Philadelphia	12-19-71	34
Kareem Abdul-Jabbar	vs Detroit	12-14-75	34
Wilt Chamberlain	vs Seattle	02-12-69	33
Wilt Chamberlain	vs Cincinnati	10-22-68	32
Wilt Chamberlain	vs Chicago	03-07-71	32
Wilt Chamberlain	vs Cincinnati	10-29-71	32
Wilt Chamberlain	vs Philadelphia	02-11-73	32

ASSISTS

Earvin Johnson	vs Denver	11-17-89	24
Earvin Johnson	vs Phoenix	01-09-90	24
Earvin Johnson	vs Dallas	04-20-88	23
Earvin Johnson	vs Seattle	04-21-84	23
Jerry West	vs Philadelphia	02-01-87	23
Earvin Johnson	vs Cleveland	11-17-84	22
Earvin Johnson	vs Boston	12-15-89	21
Earvin Johnson	vs Seattle	04-23-89	21
Earvin Johnson	vs LA Clippers	12-06-88	21
Earvin Johnson	vs Atlanta	01-15-83	21
Earvin Johnson	vs Philadelphia	11-28-88	20
Earvin Johnson	vs Denver	03-10-87	20
Earvin Johnson	vs Houston	04-06-86	20
Earvin Johnson	vs Phoenix	12-12-85	20
Earvin Johnson	vs LA Clippers	11-20-85	20
Earvin Johnson	vs Houston	12-19-84	20
Earvin Johnson	vs Atlanta	12-18-84	20
Earvin Johnson	vs New Jersey	11-25-84	20
Earvin Johnson	vs San Diego	03-09-83	20
Earvin Johnson	vs Milwaukee	01-26-83	20
Earvin Johnson	vs Philadelphia	01-05-83	20
Jerry West	vs Houston	11-07-72	20

STEALS

Jerry West	vs Seattle	12-17-73	10
Earvin Johnson	vs Phoenix	11-06-81	9
Earvin Johnson	vs Dallas	11-07-80	8
Gail Goodrich	vs Seattle	02-15-74	8
Norm Nixon	vs New Jersey	11-02-77	8

BLOCKED SHOTS

Elmore Smith	vs Portland	10-28-73	17
Elmore Smith	vs Detroit	10-26-73	14
Elmore Smith	vs Houston	11-04-73	14
Elmore Smith	vs Golden State	03-15-74	11
Kareem Abdul-Jabbar	vs Detroit	12-03-75	11
Kareem Abdul-Jabbar	vs Detroit	11-28-78	11
Kareem Abdul-Jabbar	vs Chicago	11-25-79	11

FT PERCENTAGE (Min. 15 Att.)

Jerry West	18-18	vs Detroit	11-10-65	1.000
Jerry West	18-18	vs New York	11-09-69	1.000
Earvin Johnson	16-16	vs New Jersey	01-19-87	1.000
Earvin Johnson	16-16	vs Houston	12-21-86	1.000
Jerry West	16-16	vs San Francisco	01-11-67	1.000
Jerry West	16-16	vs Baltimore	01-28-66	1.000
Earvin Johnson	15-15	vs San Antonio	11-24-89	1.000
George Mikan	15-15	vs Rochester	11-18-50	1.000
Jerry West	15-15	vs Baltimore	01-20-66	1.000
Elgin Baylor	20-21	vs St. Louis	12-21-62	952
Jerry West	20-21	vs San Fransico	01-21-66	952
George Mikan	19-20	vs Baltimore	02-26-49	950
Jerry West	19-20	vs Cincinnati	12-03-65	950
Jerry West	19-20	vs Philadelphia	12-17-65	.950

ALL-TIME TOP LAKERS PERFORMANCES (GAME)

OFFENSIVE REBOUNDS

Earvin Johnson	vs Houston	03-21-82	13
Happy Hairston	vs Seattle	02-15-74	12
Kurt Rambis	vs Golden State	03-03-86	11
Kermit Washington	vs Cleveland	11-15-77	11
Happy Hairston	vs Cleveland	11-08-73	11
A.C. Green	vs Golden State	01-06-90	11
A.C. Green	vs San Antonio	03-20-87	10
A.C. Green	vs Phoenix	03-01-86	10
Happy Hairston	vs Kansas City	03-28-75	10
Happy Hairston	vs Chicago	02-18-75	10
Elmore Smith	vs Golden State	10-18-74	10
Happy Hairston	vs Philadelphia	12-21-73	10

DEFENSIVE REBOUNDS

Kareem Abdul-Jabbar	vs Detroit	12-14-75	29
Kareem Abdul-Jabbar	vs Kansas City	11-07-76	23
Kareem Abdul-Jabbar	vs New Jersey	02-03-78	23
Kareem Abdul-Jabbar	vs Seattle	12-27-75	22
Kareem Abdul-Jabbar	vs Boston	12-28-75	22
Happy Hairston	vs Milwaukee	02-27-74	21
Kareem Abdul-Jabbar	vs Seattle	10-31-75	21
Kareem Abdul-Jabbar	vs Buffalo	11-28-75	21
Kareem Abdul-Jabbar	vs Houston	03-18-79	21
Elmore Smith	vs Seattle	10-19-73	20
Kareem Abdul-Jabbar	vs Philadelphia	12-12-75	20
Kareem Abdui-Jabbar	vs Atlanta	10-29-76	20

FG ATTEMPTS

Elgin Baylor	vs Philadelphia	12-02-61	55
Elgin Baylor	vs New York	11-15-60	48
Elgin Baylor	vs Boston	11-08-59	47
George Mikan	vs Rochester	01-20-52	45
Elgin Baylor	vs Detroit	02-16-61	45
Jerry West	vs Baltimore	04-09-65	43
Elgin Baylor	vs Detroit	02-02-65	42
George Mikan	vs New York	03-13-49	40
George Mikan	vs Rochester	11-18-50	40
Elgin Baylor	vs Cincinnati	03-04-63	40

FG MADE

Wilt Chamberlain	vs Phoenix	02-09-69	29
Elgin Baylor	vs New York	11-15-60	28
Elgin Baylor	vs Boston	11-08-59	25
Elgin Baylor	vs Detroit	02-16-61	22
Elgin Baylor	vs Philadelphia	12-02-61	22
Kareem Abdul-Jabbar	vs Houston	02-06-86	21
George Mikan	vs New York	03-13-49	21
George Mikan	vs Philadelphia	01-20-51	21
Elgin Baylor	vs New York	02-25-59	21
Elgin Baylor	vs Rochester	10-18-59	20
Jerry West	vs Cincinnati	01-17-62	20
Wilt Chamberlain	vs Detroit	01-26-69	20

FT ATTEMPTS

Wilt Chamberlain	vs Philadelphia	10-17-69	30
Larry Foust	vs St. Louis	11-30-57	26
Jerry West	vs New York	01-08-57	24
Wilt Chamberlain	vs Cincinnati	01-26-69	24
George Mikan	vs Anderson	11-19-49	23
George Mikan	vs Chicago	12-03-49	23
Jerry West	vs San Francisco	01-21-66	23

FT MADE

Larry Foust	vs St. Louis	11-30-57	22
George Mikan	vs Anderson	11-19-49	20
George Mikan	vs Chicago	12-03-49	20
Elgin Baylor	vs St Louis	12-21-62	20
Jerry West	vs San Francisco	10-30-65	20
Jerry West	vs New York	01-08-66	20
Jerry West	vs San Francisco	02-21-66	20

ALL-TIME LAKERS RECORDS (INDIVIDUAL)

FULL GAME

Most Points	Elgin Baylor	Los Angeles @ New York	11-15-60	71
Most FGA	Elgin Baylor	Los Angeles @ New York	11-15-60	46
Most FGM	Wilt Chamberlain	Phoenix vs. Los Angeles	02-09-69	29
Most FTA	Larry Foust	Minneapolis @ St. Louis	11-30-57	26
Most FTM	Larry Foust	Minneapolis @ St. Louis	11-30-57	22
Most Rebounds	Wilt Chamberlain	Los Angeles vs Boston	03-07-69	42
Most Assists	Earvin Johnson	Los Angeles vs Denver	11-17-89	24
	Earvin Johnson	Log Angeles vs Phoenix	01-09-90	24
	Jerry West	Los Angeles vs Philadelphia	02-01-67	23
	Earvin Johnson	Los Angeles vs Seattle	02-21-64	23
	Earvin Johnson	Los Angeles vs Dallas	04-20-66	23
Most Steals	Jerry West	Los Angeles vs Seattle	02-21-64	10
Most Blocked Shots	Elmore Smith	Los Angeles vs Portland	10-28-73	17

ONE HALF

Most Points	Elgin Baylor	Los Angeles @ New York	11-15-60	37
Most FGA	Elgin Baylor	Los Angeles @ New York	11-15-60	26
Most FGM	Elgin Baylor	Los Angeles @ New York	11-15-60	15
Most FTA	Jerry West	Los Angeles @ New York	10-22-63	15
	Earvin Johnson	Boston @ Los Angeles	02-17-85	15
	Earvin Johnson	Golden State@ Los Angeles	01-15-87	15
Most FTM	Jerry West	Los Angeles @ New York	10-22-63	14
	Earvin Johnson	Boston @ Los Angeles	02-17-85	14
Most Rebounds	Wilt Chamberlain	Los Angeles vs Boston	03-07-69	27
Most Assists	Earvin Johnson	Los Angeles vs Seattle	02-21-64	16
Mos t Steals	Jerry West	Los Angeles vs Seattle	12-07-73	6
Most Blocked Shots	Elmore Smith	Los Angeles vs Portland	10-28-73	10

ONE QUARTER

Most Points	Elgin Baylor	Los Angeles @ New York	11-15-60	24
	Jerry West	Los Angeles vs New York	01-17-62	24
Most FGA	Elgin Baylor	Los Angeles @ New York	11-15-60	16
Most FGM	Gail Goodrich	Los Angeles vs Baltimore	11-05-71	9
	Jerry West	Los Angeles vs New York	01-17-62	9
	Wilt Chamberlain	Los Angeles vs Phoenix	02-09-69	9
	Earl Tatum	Los Angeles vs Philadeiphia	01-26-77	9
	Magic Johnson	Los Angeles vs Golden State	04-08-83	9
Most FGM	James Worthy	Los Angeles @ Phoenix	12-13-65	9
	Kareem Abdul-Jabbar	Los Angeles @ Houston	02-06-66	9
Most FTA	Art Spoelstra	Minneapolis vs Boston	01-05-56	14
Most FTM	Gail Goodrich	Los Angeles vs Portland	10-26-73	10
Most Rebounds	Gene Wiley	Los Angeles vs New York	11-05-62	14
	Happy Hairston	Los Angeles vs Philadelphia	11-15-74	14
Most Assists	Earvin Johnson	Los Angeles vs Seattle	02-21-64	12
Most Blocked Shots	Elmore Smith	Los Angeles vs Portland	10-26-73	6

ALL-TIME LAKERS RECORDS (TEAM)

FULL GAME

Most Points	Los Angeles vs. Golden State	03-19-72	162
Most FGA	Minneapolis @ Boston	02-27-59	153
Most FGM	Los Angeles vs Golden State	03-19-72	69
Most FTA	Minneapolis vs Philadelphia	11-02-57	64
Most FTM	Minneapolis vs Baltimore	1949	51
	Minneapolis vs St Louis	1957	51
Most Rebounds	Los Angeles vs Philadelphia	12-08-61	90
Most Assists	Los Angeles vs Denver	02-23-82	51
Most Steals	Los Angeles vs Kansas City	11-09-82	23

ONE HALF

Most Points	Los Angeles vs Chicago	01-23-66	91
	Los Angeles vs Golden State	03-19-72	91
Most FGA	Minneapolis @ Boston	02-27-59	73
Most FGM	Los Angeles vs Golden State	03-19-72	37
	Los Angeles vs Denver	02-23-62	37
Most FTA	Minneapolis @ Philadelphia	02-15-57	42
Most FTM	Minneapolis @ Philadelpnia	02-15-57	32
Most Rebounds	Los Angeles @ Detroit	01-09-66	SS
Most Assists	Los Angeles vs Detroit	11-24-72	28

ONE QUARTER

Most Points	Los Angeles vs Detroit	03-31-62	51
Most FGA	Minneapolis @ Boston	02-27-59	39
Most FGM	Los Angeles vs Chicago	01-23-66	22
Most FTA	Los Angeles vs Chicago	01-25-66	27
Most FTM	Los Angeles vs Chicago	01-25-66	21
	Los Angeles vs Philadeiphia	12-19-71	21
Most Rebounds	Los Angeles vs St. Louis	02-21-60	31
Most Assists	Los Angeles vs Denver	02-23-82	17

LAKERS ALL-TIME SCORING

Player	GP	FGM	FGA	PCT	FTM	FTA	PCT	REB	AST	PF	PTS	AVG
Abernethy	143	370	752	.491	192	245	.748	556	199	240	932	6.5
Abdul-Jabbar	1093	9935	17520	.567	4305	5932	.726	10279	3652	3224	24176	22.1
Alcorn	19	12	39	.308	7	8	.875	46	2	44	31	1.6
Allen	210	1376	3045	.452	599	775	.773	712	1081	618	3351	15 9
Anderson	18	7	29	.241	12	28	.429	11	17	18	26	1.4
Barnes	122	318	732	.434	187	275	.660	661	74	400	823	6.7
Barnett	232	1463	3267	.448	964	1213	.795	692	621	631	3890	16.6
Bates	4	2	16	.125	1	2	.500	1	0	1	5	1 3
Baylor	846	8693	20173	.431	5763	7390	.780	11463	3650	2596	23149	27.4
Beaty	69	136	310	.439	108	135	.800	327	74	130	380	5.5
Block	22	20	52	.385	24	34	.706	45	5	20	64	2.9
Boone	252	1563	3457	.457	742	872	.852	746	610	164	3906	15.5
Boozer	76	365	754	.484	225	289	.779	548	87	196	955	12.2
Branch	32	48	96	.500	42	54	.778	53	16	39	138	4.3
Brewer	149	182	372	.489	22	59	.372	545	97	285	387	2 6
Brickowski	37	53	94	.564	40	59	.678	97	12	105	146	3.9
Bridges	82	333	722	.461	197	255	.702	904	219	296	645	10.3
Brown	1	0	0	.000	1	3	.333	0	0	1	1	1.0
Bucknall	23	9	33	.273	5	6	.833	7	10	10	23	1.5
Byrnes	32	25	50	.500	13	15	.867	27	13	32	63	2 0
Calhoun	133	292	654	.446	109	145	.752	577	160	376	693	5.2
Calvin	12	27	82	.329	41	48	.854	16	21	16	95	7.9
Campbell	76	215	446	.462	98	122	.803	157	62	149	531	7.0
Carr	129	366	768	.476	140	224	.622	517	67	285	872	6.9
Carter, B.	54	114	247	.462	70	95	.737	65	52	99	301	5.6
Carter, R.	46	54	124	.435	36	54	.667	45	25	54	144	3.1
Carty	28	34	89	.382	8	11	.727	58	11	31	76	2.7
Chamberlain	339	2360	3902	.605	1265	2662	.475	6524	1461	734	5985	17.7
Chambers	69	224	496	.452	68	93	.731	208	44	143	516	7 5
Chaney	90	226	558	.405	75	10	.750	341	325	238	527	5.9
Chones	164	750	1151	.496	251	362	.693	1221	304	595	1751	10.7
Clark	157	959	2041	.470	492	673	.731	560	558	428	2410	15.4
Cleamons	38	35	100	.350	28	36	.778	39	35	21	98	2.6
Cooper, J.	2	1	4	.250	0	0	.000	2	0	3	2	1.0
Cooper, M.	873	3014	6429	.469	1273	1529	.833	2769	3666	2329	7729	8.9
Counts	334	1442	3245	.444	603	788	.765	2447	494	1039	3509	10.5
Crawford	119	370	784	.472	157	274	.573	327	249	328	897	7.5
Dantley	116	851	1458	.584	626	759	.825	746	326	330	2128	18.3
Davis	38	38	83	.457	25	33	.758	36	92	49	101	2.7
DiGregorio	25	41	100	.410	16	20	.800	23	71	22	98	3.9
Edwards	25	145	316	.459	80	125	.640	180	29	89	370	14.8
Egan	154	461	1088	.424	303	361	.839	251	431	377	1225	8.0
Ellis, B.	118	227	564	.402	153	220	.695	616	86	201	607	5.1
Ellis, L.	402	1275	2970	.429	699	1012	.691	2746	259	943	3249	6.1
Erickson	309	1230	2754	.447	391	526	.743	1392	903	854	2851	9.2
Fairchild	30	23	89	.258	14	20	.700	45	11	33	60	2.0
Felix	205	496	1295	.383	295	435	.678	1350	115	745	1287	6.3
Finkel	27	17	47	.362	7	12	.583	64	5	39	41	1.5
Ford	368	1139	2436	.467	340	448	.756	1405	523	865	2616	7.6
Freeman	64	263	606	.434	163	199	.819	180	171	160	689	10.8
Garrett, C.	41	78	152	.457	30	39	.769	71	31	62	188	4.6
Garrett, D.	73	354	816	.434	138	162	.852	234	180	236	846	11.6
Gibson	9	6	20	.300	12	24	.500	4	6	10	13	1.4
Goodrich	687	4493	11098	.405	2830	3466	.817	2081	2863	1865	13044	19.0
Grant	33	51	116	.440	23	26	.885	52	7	19	125	3.8
Grote	11	6	11	.545	2	2	1.000	4	4	4	14	1.3
Gudmundsson	8	20	37	.541	18	27	.667	38	3	25	58	7.3
Hairston	395	2182	4524	.482	1629	2074	.785	4885	920	1260	5993	15.2
Hardy	22	22	59	.373	7	10	.700	19	3	13	51	2.3
Hamilton	44	54	108	.500	13	13	1.000	72	30	46	21	2.8
Hawkins, C.	114	507	1057	.480	241	323	.746	720	499	319	1255	11.0
Hawkins, T.	457	1723	3823	.451	658	1173	.561	2569	517	1305	4084	8.9
Hawthorne	33	38	93	.409	30	48	.625	32	23	33	106	3.2
Haywood	76	288	591	.487	159	206	.772	346	93	197	736	9.7
Hazzard	225	876	2015	.435	357	505	.707	561	856	559	2109	9.4
Henderson	1	2	3	.667	0	0	.000	1	0	1	4	4.0
Hetzel	59	111	256	.421	60	77	.779	149	37	99	282	4.8
Hewitt	95	264	616	.429	77	137	.562	473	104	178	605	6.4
Higgins	6	0	0	.000	1	2	.500	1	1	4	1	0.3
Holland	79	91	215	.423	50	65	.769	46	40	68	236	3.0
Hoover	4	2	3	.667	0	0	.000	3	1	3	4	1.0
Horn	28	27	82	.329	20	29	.690	61	20	46	74	2.6
Hudson	160	822	1628	.505	247	301	.821	328	334	329	1891	11.8
Hundley	432	1382	3978	.347	861	1195	.721	1420	1455	786	3625	8.4
Imhoff	316	959	2041	.470	469	783	.600	2952	628	1017	2387	7.6
Jackson	2	1	3	.333	0	0	.000	2	2	1	2	1.0
Johnson, C.	55	64	155	.413	41	54	.759	81	31	75	169	3.1
Johnson, R.	14	13	43	.302	11	17	.647	29	3	10	37	2.6

LAKERS ALL-TIME SCORING (CONTINUED)

Player	GP	FGM	FGA	PCT	FTM	FTA	PCT	REB	AST	PF	PTS	AVG
Joliff	46	46	141	326	11	23	.478	141	16	53	103	2.2
Jones, D.	32	62	132	.470	32	48	.667	114	22	82	156	4.9
Jones, E.	2	0	1	.000	O	O	.000	O	O	O	O	0.0
Jordan	156	253	627	.404	117	166	.705	153	411	291	631	4.0
Killum	4	0	4	.000	1	1	1.000	2	0	1	1	0.3
King	213	506	1212	.417	278	367	.757	531	511	473	1290	6.1
Krebs	515	1700	4192	.406	740	979	.756	3180	428	1537	4140	8.0
Kupchak	173	441	876	.503	231	335	.690	672	78	332	1113	6.4
Kupec	98	163	382	.427	85	112	.759	222	58	120	411	4.2
Lamar	71	228	561	.406	46	68	.672	92	177	73	502	7.1
Lamp	40	27	69	.391	6	7	.684	34	15	28	62	1.6
Landsberger	206	417	895	.466	136	262	.519	1069	85	344	970	4.7
Lantz	109	274	650	.422	225	265	.849	269	234	239	773	7.1
LaRusso	583	2947	6785	.434	2337	3098	.754	5471	1216	1803	8231	14.1
Lee	11	4	13	.308	6	7	.857	8	9	2	14	1.3
Leonard	324	1067	3137	.340	718	962	.746	950	906	645	2852	8.8
Lester	59	60	134	.448	36	50	.720	36	134	52	156	2.6
Love	81	204	472	.432	96	130	.738	267	74	201	504	6.2
Lucas	77	302	653	.462	180	230	.783	566	84	253	785	10.2
Lynn	44	44	133	.331	31	48	.646	64	30	87	119	2.7
McAdoo	224	1079	2186	.494	543	715	.759	990	212	614	2706	12.1
McCarter	116	379	941	.403	89	137	.650	205	219	223	847	7.3
McDaniels	35	41	102	.402	9	9	1 000	74	15	40	91	2.6
McGee	302	1077	2075	.519	245	413	.593	600	277	563	2465	8.2
McGill	8	7	20	.350	1	11	.000	12	3	6	15	1.9
McKenna	36	26	87	.322	11	17	.647	29	14	45	67	1.9
McMillan	242	1586	3391	.468	542	671	.808	1299	563	507	3714	15.3
McNelll	50	56	136	.412	26	34	.765	56	89	56	138	2.9
Mack	27	21	50	.420	9	18	.500	22	20	18	51	1.9
Matthews	101	203	435	.487	83	101	.822	113	238	118	497	4.9
Meely	20	20	51	.392	24	32	.750	45	9	30	64	3.2
Mlx	1	4	10	.400	1	1	1.000	1	2	1	9	9.0
Mueller	39	132	254	.520	61	103	.592	222	78	86	325	8.3
Murphy	2	1	5	.200	3	7	.429	4	0	5	5	2.5
Nash	25	14	57	.246	25	32	.781	35	10	30	53	2.1
Nater	69	124	253	.490	63	91	.692	264	27	150	311	4.5
Nelson	119	171	408	.419	169	227	.744	396	100	221	511	4.3
Neumann	59	146	363	.402	54	81	.667	63	137	127	346	5.9
Nevitt	15	8	28	.286	6	14	.429	27	5	26	22	1.5
Nixon	485	3480	6963	.500	972	1262	.770	1312	3846	1416	7938	16.4
Oldham	3	2	3	.667	1	2	.500	1	1	3	5	1.7
Patrick	3	2	5	.400	1	2	.500	2	1	3	5	1.7
Price, J.	225	942	2067	.456	343	431	.796	659	747	512	2227	9.9
Rambis	493	1022	1849	.553	564	824	.684	2911	435	1221	2608	5.3
Reed	46	33	91	.363	10	15	.667	107	23	73	76	1.7
Riley	369	1558	3596	.433	648	826	.785	673	918	859	3764	10.2
Rlvers	47	49	122	.402	35	42	.833	43	106	50	134	2 9
Roberson	139	387	887	.436	208	355	.588	978	139	381	982	7.1
Roberts	28	27	76	.355	4	6	.667	25	19	34	58	2.1
Robinson	70	276	563	.490	117	137	.854	122	146	150	669	9.6
Robisch	135	254	585	.434	136	180	.756	464	137	179	644	4.8
Roche	15	3	14	.214	2	4	.500	3	6	7	8	0.5
Russell	198	1212	2561	.474	421	480	.877	592	441	341	2847	14.5
Scott	48	225	509	.442	110	142	.775	148	235	155	560	11.7
Selvy	409	1470	3657	.402	978	1369	.714	1413	1203	869	3918	9.6
Sims	18	21	59	.356	19	32	.594	27	12	40	61	3.4
Smith, E.	155	780	1651	.472	259	480	.540	1716	295	534	1819	11.7
Smith, R.	3	0	1	.000	O	O	.000	O	0	1	0	0 .0
Smrek	83	74	163	.454	60	91	.659	122	13	175	208	2.5
Spriggs	156	326	628	.519	186	245	.759	369	211	328	838	5.4
Tatum	93	436	921	.473	117	159	.736	326	188	253	989	10.6
Thompson, B.	68	145	274	.529	56	84	.667	180	61	159	346	5.1
Tolbert	14	16	28	.571	10	13	.769	20	5	14	42	3.0
Trapp	63	142	326	.436	58	83	.699	194	44	140	342	5.4
Tresvant	28	65	123	.528	30	45	.667	88	27	51	160	5.7
Turner	19	17	52	.327	4	7	.571	25	11	13	38	2.0
Wagner	40	62	147	.422	26	29	.897	28	61	42	152	3.8
Warner	95	276	577	.478	93	134	.694	791	117	311	645	6.8
Washington	214	500	1072	.466	343	534	.642	1433	183	565	1343	6.3
Wesley	1	1	2	.500	2	4	.500	1	1	2	4	4.0
West	932	9016	19032	.474	7160	8801	.814	5376	6238	2435	25192	27.0
Wetzel	38	51	119	.437	35	46	.761	84	51	55	139	3.7
Wiley	299	551	1188	.472	167	330	.506	2188	252	811	1269	4.2
Wilkes	575	4533	8790	.516	1529	2029	.754	3119	1474	1611	10601	18 4
Williams	9	17	43	.395	10	13	.769	19	21	15	44	4 9
Winters	68	359	810	.443	76	92	.926	138	195	168	794	11.7
Woolridge	136	537	1044	.514	429	583	.736	455	161	290	1503	11.1
Yates	37	31	105	.295	10	22	.454	94	16	72	72	1.9

BIGGEST LAKERS WINS

Team	Margin	Score	Location	Date
Atlanta	44	(139- 90)	@ Atlanta	01-07-72
Boston	40	(144-104)	@ Boston	02-11-68
Charlotte	33	(123- 90)	@ Charlotte	03-10-89
Chicago	27	(132-105)	@ Chicago	02-15-68
Cleveland	43	(127- 84)	@ LA	03-04-73
Dallas	25	(118- 93)	@ Dallas	01-29-89
Denver	38	(147-109)	@ LA	01-07-87
Detroit	56	(144- 88)	@ LA	11-12-66
Golden State	63	(162- 99)	@ LA	03-19-72
Houston	36	(152-116)	@ LA	10-27-68
Indiana	28	(134-106)	@ LA	11-12-78
LA Clippers	46	(137- 91)	@ S.D.	11-13-79
Miami	47	(138- 91)	@ Miami	11-23-88
Milwaukee	29	(126- 97)	@ LA	11-15-83
Minnesota	24	(113- 89)	@ LA	04-19-90
New Jersey	24	(124-100)	@ LA	04-08-77
	24	(147-123)	@ LA	11-25-83
New York	29	(152-123)	@ LA	01-15-66
Orlando	15	(121-106)	@ LA	01-10-90
Philadelphia	40	(143-103)	@ Phil	11-10-71
	40	(135- 95)	@ LA	11-19-72
Phoenix	37	(144-107)	@ Phoenix	10-31-85
	37	(155-118)	@ LA	01-02-87
Portland	36	(137-101)	@ LA	12-10-72
	36	(140-104)	@ Portland	01-01-87
Sacramento	44	(146-102)	@ LA	02-06-68
San Antonio	40	(138- 98)	@ LA	03-30-89
Seattle	38	(151-113)	@ LA	02-02-68
Utah	46	(130- 84)	@ LA	03-05-86
Washington	33	(131- 98)	@ LA	11-04-66

WORST LAKERS LOSSES

Team	Margin	Score	Location	Date
Atlanta	37	(101-138)	@ LA	11-01-59
Boston	34	(139-173)	@ Boston	02-27-59
Chicago	23	(105-128)	@ Chicago	02-18-75
Cleveland	20	(103-123)	@ LA	12-16-75
Dallas	23	(104-127)	@ LA	04-13-88
Denver	16	(130-146)	@ LA	11-06-85
Detroit	35	(100-135)	@ Detroit	01-25-79
Golden State	39	(93-132)	@ S. Fran.	11-11-66
Houston	32	(104-136)	@ Houston	12-27-68
Indiana	13	(98-111)	@ Indiana	12-08-76
LA Clippers	33	(101-134)	@ LA	11-03-74
Milwaukee	34	(88-122)	@ Milw.	02-05-71
New Jersey	15	(106 121)	@ NJ	02-21-86
New York	33	(82-115)	@ New York	03-16-71
Orlando	5	(103-108)	@ Orlando	12-10-89
Philadelphia	30	(128-158)	@ Phil.	03-18-68
Phoenix	35	(100-135)	@ Phoenix	12-25-73
Portland	42	(88-130)	@ Portland	04-22-90
Sacramento	34	(112-146)	@ Omaha	01-05-71
San Antonio	32	(103-135)	@ S A.	02-22-77
Seattle	24	(105-129)	@ Seattle	12-26-73
	24	(89-113)	@ Seattle	11-24-77
	24	(101-125)	@ Seattle	01-28-87
Utah	26	(79-105)	@ Utah	02-22-89
Washington	32	(97-129)	@ LA	11-23-69

ALL-TIME LAKERS COACHES

Coach	Titles Won	Regular Season Won-Lost	Pct.	Playoffs Won-Lost	Pct.	Totals Won-Lost	Pct.	Years Coached
John Kundla	5	423-302	.583	60-35	.632	483-337	.589	1948-1959
George Mikan	0	9-30	.231	—	—	9-30	.231	1957-1958
John Castellani	0	11-25	.306	—	—	11-25	.306	1959-1960
Jim Pollard	0	14-25	.359	5-4	.556	19-29	.396	1959-1960
Fred Schaus	0	315-245	.563	33-38	.465	348-283	.552	1960-1967
Bill Van Breda Kolff	0	107-57	.652	21-12	.636	128-69	.650	1967-1969
Joe Mullaney	0	94-70	.573	16-14	.533	110-84	.567	1969-1971
Bill Sharman	1	246-164	.600	22-15	.595	268-179	.600	1971-1976
Jerry West	0	145-101	.589	8-14	.364	153-115	.571	1976-1979
Jack McKinney	0	9-4	.714	—	—	9-4	.714	1979-1980
Paul Westhead	1	113-49	.697	13-5	.723	126-54	.700	1979-1981
Pat Riley	4	533-194	.733	102-47	.685	635-241	.725	1981-1990
Minneapolis Totals	**5**	**457-382**	**.545**	**65-39**	**.625**	**522-421**	**.554**	
Los Angeles Totals	**6**	**1561-887**	**.638**	**215-146**	**.596**	**1719-1008**	**.630**	
LAKERS TOTALS	**11**	**2018-1269**	**.614**	**280-185**	**.602**	**2298-1454**	**.613**	

BIGGEST HEADACHES FOR THE LAKERS

POINTS
(Those who have scored 45 points or more in a game)

Wilt Chamberlain	Philadelphia @ Philadelphia	12-08-61	78
Wilt Chamberlain	San Francisco @ Los Angeles	11-03-62 (3 OT)	72
Wilt Chamberlain	San Francisco @ San Francisco	01-17-63	67
Wilt Chamberlain	Philadelphia @ Philadelphia	02-07-66	65
Wilt Chamberlain	San Francisco @ San Francisco	12-14-62	63
Wilt Chamberlain	Philadelphia @ Los Angeles	12-01-61	60
Wilt Chamberlain	Philadelphia @ Philadelphia	12-29-61	60
Jack Twyman	Cincinn. vs Minneapolis @ Cincinnati	01-15-60	59
Wilt Chamberlain	San Francisco @ San Francisco	12-06-63	59
Wilt Chamberlain	Philadelphia @ Philadelphia	12-20-61	57
Wilt Chamberlain	Philadelphia @ Philadelphia	01-21-61	56
Earl Monroe	Baltimore @ Baltimore	02-13-68	56
Wilt Chamberlain	Philadelphia @ Philadelphia	11-12-61	56
Wilt Chamberlain	San Francisco @ Los Angeles	02-16-63	56
Oscar Robertson	Cincinnati @ Cincinnati	12-18-64	56
Wilt Chamberlain	San Francisco @ Los Angeles	11-02-63	55
Wilt Chamberlain	San Francisco @ Los Angeles	03-14-64	55
Willis Reed	New York @ New York	11-01-67	53
Wilt Chamberlain	Philadelphia @ Philadelphia	03-18-68	53
Kareem Abdul-Jabbar	Milwaukee @ Los Angeles	03-17-73	50
Rick Barry	San Francisco @ San Francisco	12-08-73	50
Adrian Dantley	Utah @ Utah	11-27-79	50
John Drew	Atlanta @ Los Angeles	02-12-78	48
Bob McAdoo	Buffalo @ Los Angeles	02-11-75	47
Bob Rule	Seattle @ Seattle	11-21-67	47
Lloyd Free	San Diego @ San Diego	10-12-79	46
Pete Maravich	New Orleans @ Los Angeles	03-20-77	46
Lew Alcindor	Milwaukee @ Milwaukee	01-14-70	46
Andrew Toney	Philadelphia @ Philadelphia	03-07-82	46
Bob McAdoo	New York @ Los Angeles	01-23-79	45
Bob Rule	Seattle @ Los Angeles	12-14-69	45
Dave Bing	Detroit @ Los Angeles	03-17-68	45
Alex English	Denver @ Los Angeles	11-21-82	45
Karl Malone	Utah @ Utah	04-12-90	45

REBOUNDS
(Those who have grabbed 25 or more rebounds in a game)

Wilt Chamberlain	Philadelphia @ Philadelphia	01-21-61	45
Wilt Chamberlain	Philadelphia @ Philadelphia	12-08-61 (3 OT)	44
Bill Russell	Boston @ Boston	01-20-63	43
Wilt Chamberlain	Philadelphia @ New York	11-29-60	38
Bill Russell	Boston @ Boston	03-03-65	38
Nate Thurmond	San Francisco @ Los Angeles	02-02-69	34
Bill Russell	Boston @ Boston	11-03-67	33
Wilt Chamberlain	Philadelphia @ Philadelphia	03-18-68	32
Wilt Chamberlain	Philadelphia @ Philadelphia	10-18-67	30
Elvin Hayes	San Diego @ San Diego	12-05-70	30
George T. Johnson	Golden State @ Los Angeles	03-15-74	30
Jim Fox	Seattle @ Seattle	12-26-73	30
Nate Thurmond	Golden State @ Golden State	12-29-73	29
Jerry Lucas	San Francisco @ Los Angeles	03-10-70	28
Walt Bellamy	Atlanta @ Atlanta	03-03-70	27
Len Robinson	New Orleans @ Los Angeles	11-11-77	27
Sidney Wicks	Portland @ Los Angeles	02-26-75	27
Len Robinson	New Orleans @ New Orleans	12-13-77	26
Bill Walton	Portland @ Portland	12-18-76	26
Elvin Hayes	San Diego @ San Diego	12-23-69	26
Rich Kelley	New Orleans @ Los Angeles	11-17-78	25
John Drew	Atlanta @ Atlanta	12-28-74	25
Elvin Hayes	Capital @ Capital	11-21-73	25
Spencer Haywood	Seattle @ Seattle	03-25-73	25

LAKERS TOP SCORING PERFORMANCES

Elgin Baylor	@	New York	11-15-60	71
Wilt Chamberlin	@	Phoenix	02-09-69	66
Elgin Baylor	vs	Boston	11-08-59	64
Elgin Baylor	@	Philadelphia	12-08-61	63
Jerry West	vs	New York	01-17-62	63
George Mikan	vs	Rochester	01-20-52	61
Wilt Chamberlain	vs	Cincinnati	01-26-69	60
Elgin Baylor	@	Detroit	02-16-61	57
Elgin Baylor	vs	Syracuse	01-24-61	56
Elgin Baylor	vs	Cincinnati (@ Detroit)	02-25-59	55
George Mikan	vs	Baltimore	02-26-49	53
Jerry West	vs	Cincinnati	01-29-65	53
Gail Goodrich	vs	Kansas City-Omaha	03-28-75	53
Elgin Baylor	vs	Detroit	10-18-59	52
Elgin Baylor	vs	Detroit (@ San Francisco)	11-20-60	52
Elgin Baylor	vs	Philadelphia (@ Hershey)	12-08-61	52
Elgin Baylor	vs	St. Louis	12-11-61	52
Elgin Baylor	vs	St. Louis	12-13-61	52
Elgin Baylor	vs	San Francisco	12-15-62	52
George Mikan	vs	New York	03-13-49	51
George Mikan	@	Rochester	01-14-50	51
Elgin Baylor	@	Detroit	11-25-60	51
Elgin Baylor	@	San Francisco	12-14-62	51
Jerry West	vs	Cincinnati	12-03-65	51
Jerry West	@	Cincinnati	12-10-65	51
Elgin Baylor	vs	Syracuse	12-04-61	50
Jerry West	vs	Cincinnati	01-24-62	50
Rudy LaRusso	vs	St. Louis	03-14-62	50
Elgin Baylor	vs	Syracuse	12-12-62	50
Elgin Baylor	vs	Boston	02-13-63	50

LAKERS TOP REBOUNDING PERFORMANCES

Wilt Chamberlain	vs	Boston	03-07-69	42
Wilt Chamberlain	vs	Baltimore	03-09-69	38
George Mikan	vs	Rochester	01-20-52	36
George Mikan	@	Philadelphia	03-04-52	36
Wilt Chamberlain	vs	San Francisco	02-02-69	35
Wilt Chamberlain	vs	Philadelphia	12-19-71	34
Kareem Abdul-Jabbar	vs	Detroit	12-14-75	34
Wilt Chamberlain	@	Seattle	02-12-69	33
Wilt Chamberlain	@	Cincinnati	10-22-68	32
Wilt Chamberlain	@	Chicago	10-16-70	31
Wilt Chamberlain	vs	San Diego	11-29-70	31
Wilt Chamberlain	vs	Boston	11-14-71	31
Wilt Chamberlain	vs	Detroit	11-26-71	31
Wilt Chamberlain	vs	Philadelphia	02-11-73	31
Wilt Chamberlain	@	Portland	02-17-73	31
Elgin Baylor	vs	Cincinnati	01-14-61	30
Wilt Chamberlain	@	San Francisco	02-01-69	30
Wilt Chamberlain	vs	Boston	02-20-72	30

ALL-TIME LAKERS HIGHS & LOWS VS OPPONENTS

	HIGH				LOW		
Atlanta	141	@ Los Angeles	02-14-86	Atlanta	79	@ Rochester	11-10-55
Boston	144	@ Boston	02-11-68	Boston	82	@ Boston	01-10-69
					82	@ Boston	03-10-74
Charlotte	123	@ Charlotte	03-10-89	Charlotte	114	@ Los Angeles	01-27-89
Chicago	154	@ Los Angeles	11-23-66	Chicago	76	@ Los Angeles	11-17-74
Cleveland	153	@ Cleveland	01-29-80	Cleveland	85	@ Cleveland	03-13-75
Dallas	138	@ Los Angeles	03-14-82	Dallas	96	@ Dallas	10-28-84
Denver	153	@ Los Angeles	04-09-82	Denver	95	@ Denver	03-15-77
Detroit	148	@ Los Angeles	03-24-85	Detroit	81	@ Minneapolis	11-22-50
Golden State	162	@ Los Angeles	03-19-72	Golden State	76	@ New York	11- -54
Houston	152	@ Los Angeles	10-27-68	Houston	83	@ Houston	03-05-89
Indiana	139	@ Los Angeles	03-03-89	Indiana	97	@ Indiana	01-15-82
LA Clippers	156	@ Los Angeles	03-23-79	LA Clippers	92	@ San Diego	12-16-80
Miami	138	@ Miami	11-23-88	Miami	118	@ Los Angeles	01-06-89
Milwaukee	137	@ Milwaukee	11-14-78	Milwaukee	81	@ Milwaukee	11-26-69
Minnesota	115	@ Los Angeles	03-04-90	Minnesota	101	@ Minnesota	03-17-90
New Jersey	147	@ Los Angeles	11-25-83	New Jersey	84	@ New York	03-13-77
New York	152	@ Los Angeles	01-15-66	New York	80	@ Los Angeles	12- -54
Orlando	121	@ Los Angeles	01-10-90	Orlando	103	@ Orlando	12-10-89
Philadelphia	154	@ Los Angeles	12-19-71	Philadelphia	65	@ Minneapolis	01-29-53
Phoenix	155	@ Los Angeles	01-02-87	Phoenix	88	@ Phoenix	12-07-74
Portland	153	@ Los Angeles	01-30-72	Portland	82	@ Los Angeles	10-19-79
Sacramento	146	@ Los Angeles	02-06-68	Sacramento	76	@ Philadelphia	01-09-55
San Antonio	147	@ San Antonio	03-20-87	San Antonio	84	@ Los Angeles	01-29-90
	147	@ Los Angeles	11-15-87				
Seattle	154	@ Los Angeles	01-21-68	Seattle	85	@ Seattle	11-24-87
Utah	131	@ Utah	12-04-86	Utah	79	@ Utah	02-20-89
Washington	151	@ Los Angeles	02-06-76	Washington	88	@ Washington	02-15-76

ALL-TIME OPPONENTS HIGHS & LOWS VS LAKERS

	HIGH				LOW		
Atlanta	138	@ Los Angeles	11-01-59	Atlanta	67	@ Rochester	11-10-55
Boston	173	@ Boston	02-27-59	Boston	73	@ Boston	03-16-69
Charlotte	102	@ Charlotte	12-12-89	Charlotte	89	@ Charlotte	12-12-89
Chicago	134	@ Chicago	10-19-66	Chicago	84	@ Los Angeles	11-28-76
Cleveland	154	@ Cleveland	01-29-80	Cleveland	83	@ Cleveland	10-15-72
Dallas	133	@ Los Angeles	12-02-83	Dallas	89	@ Los Angeles	01-06-88
Denver	148	@ Los Angeles	03-28-81	Denver	83	@ Los Angeles	12-12-76
Detroit	135	@ Los Angeles	02-22-72	Detroit	79	@ Minneapolis	11-22-50
	135	@ Detroit	01-25-79	Golden State	74	@ New York	10- -50
Golden State	144	@ Los Angeles	11-19-66	Houston	83	@ Los Angeles	12-22-74
Houston	136	@ Houston	12-27-72	Indiana	81	@ Indianapolis	02-19-86
Indiana	126	@ Los Angeles	03-10-84	LA Clippers	82	@ Los Angeles	11-12-87
LA Clippers	134	@ Los Angeles	11-03-74	Miami	75	@ Miami	12-13-89
Miami	108	@ Los Angeles	04-16-89	Milwaukee	82	@ Los Angeles	02-25-73
Milwaukee	130	@ Los Angeles	03-21-76	Minnesota	89	@ Los Angeles	04-19-90
Minnesota	99	@ Minesota	03-17-90	New Jersey	81	@ New Jersey	12-08-87
New Jersey	123	@ Los Angeles	11-25-83	New York	73	@ Los Angeles	12-19-54
New York	140	@ New York	02-12-65	Orlando	106	@ Los Angeles	01-10-90
Orlando	108	@ Orlando	12-10-89	Philadelphia	65	@ Syracuse	11-05-53
Philadelphia	158	@ Philadelphia	03-18-68	Phoenix	86	@ Los Angeles	12-08-82
Phoenix	138	@ Phoenix	01-19-84	Portland	81	@ Portland	01-03-88
Portland	145	@ Portland	04-09-77	Sacramento	78	@ Rochester	03-12-55
Sacramento	146	@ Omaha	01-05-71	San Antonio	96	@ Los Angeles	11-25-81
San Antonio	137	@ San Antonio	04-03-84		96´	@ Los Angeles	01-08-89
Seattle	137	@ Seattle	11-21-67	Seattle	87	@ Los Angeles	01-09-81
Utah	130	@ Los Angeles	11-22-83	Utah	84	@ Los Angeles	03-05-86
Washington	143	@ Los Angeles	01-25-74	Washington	84	@ Washington	10-22-76
					84	@ Washington	12-21-86

ALL-TIME LAKERS HONORS & AWARDS

MOST VALUABLE PLAYER—MAURICE PODOLOFF TROPHY

1975-76—Kareem Abdul-Jabbar (LA)
1976-77—Kareem Abdul-Jabbar (LA)
1979-80—Kareem Abdul Jabbar (LA)

1986-87—Earvin Johnson (LA)
1988-89—Earvin Johnson (LA)
1988-89—Earvin Johnson (LA)

ALL-NBA FIRST TEAM SELECTIONS

1948-49— George Mikan (Minn)
Jim Pollard (Minn)
1949-50— George Mikan (Minn)
Jim Pollard (Minn)
1950-51— George Mikan (Minn)
1951-52— George Mikan (Minn)
1952-53— George Mikan (Minn)
1953-54— George Mikan (Minn)
1958-59— Elgin Baylor (Minn)
1959-60— Elgin Baylor (Minn)
1960-61— Elgin Baylor (LA)
1961-62— Elgin Baylor (LA)
Jerry West (LA)
1962-63— Elgin Baylor (LA)
Jerry West (LA)
1963-64— Elgin Baylor (LA)
Jerry West (LA)
1964-65— Elgin Baylor (LA)
Jerry West (LA)
1965-66— Jerry West (LA)
1966-67— Elgin Baylor (LA)
Jerry West (LA)

1967-68— Elgin Baylor (LA)
1968-69— Elgin Baylor (LA)
1969-70— Jerry West (LA)
1970-71— Jerry West (LA)
1971-72— Jerry West (LA)
1972-73— Jerry West (LA)
1973-74— Gail Goodrich (LA)
1975-76— Kareem Abdul-Jabbar (LA)
1976-77— Kareem Abdul-Jabbar (LA)
1979-80— Kareem Abdul-Jabbar (LA)
1980-81— Kareem Abdul-Jabbar (LA)
1982-83— Earvin Johnson (LA)
1983-84— Kareem Abdul-Jabbar (LA)
Earvin Johnson (LA)
1984-85— Earvin Johnson (LA)
1985-86— Kareem Abdul-Jabbar (LA)
Earvin Johnson (LA)
1986-87— Earvin Johnson (LA)
1987-88— Earvin Johnson (LA)
1988-89— Earvin Johnson (LA)
1989-90— Earvin Johnson (LA)

LAKERS ALL-TIME PLAYOFF HIGHS

Points	vs.	Denver	05-22-85	153
Field Goals Made	vs.	Denver	05-22-85	67
Field Goals Attempted	@	Detroit	03-18-61	116
	vs.	Denver	05-22-85	116
Shooting Percentage	vs.	San Antonio	04-17-86	.663
Free Throws Made	vs.	Denver	04-25-87	49
Free Throws Attempted	@	Atlanta	04-12-70	60
Free Throws Percentage	vs.	Dallas	06-04-88	.955
Rebounds	vs.	St. Louis	03-24-61	81
Assists	vs.	Phoenix	04-09-70	44
	vs.	New York	05-06-70	44
	vs.	Boston	06-04-87	44

LAKERS ALL-TIME PLAYOFF LOWS

Points	vs.	Milwaukee	04-09-72	72
Field Goals Made	vs.	Milwaukee	04-09-72	28
	@	Milwaukee	04-11-71	28
Field Goals Attempted	@	New York	05-04-72	66
Field Goal Percentage	vs.	Milwaukee	04-09-72	.272
Free Throws Made	@	Philadelphia	05-26-83	3
Free Throws Attempted	@	Philadelphia	05-26-83	5
Free Throw Percentage	@	Milwaukee	04-09-71	.481
Rebounds	vs.	Dallas	05-25-88	28

OPPONENTS ALL-TIME PLAYOFF HIGHS

Points	Los Angeles	@ Boston	05-27-85	148
Field Goals Made	Los Angeles	@ Boston	05-27-85	62
Field Goals Attempted	Los Angeles	@ St. Louis	03-21-61	125
Shooting Percentage	Milwaukee	@ Los Angeles	04-16-71	.619
Free Throws Made	Boston	@ Los Angeles	04-26-66	43
	Los Angeles	@ Boston	06-12-84	43
Free Throws Attempted	Boston	@ Los Angeles	04-26-66	55
Free Throw Percentage	Houston	@ Los Angeles	04-05-81	.955
Rebounds	Los Angeles	@ Boston	04-18-62	82
Assists	Los Angeles	@ Boston	05-27-85	43

OPPONENTS ALL-TIME PLAYOFF LOW

Points	Los Angeles @ Golden State	04-21-73	70
Field Goals Made	Los Angeles @ Golden State	04-21-73	27
Field Goals Attempted	Detroit @ Los Angeles	06-13-89	70
Shooting Percentage	Los Angeles @ Golden State	04-21-73	.233
Free Throws Made	Los Angeles @ Seattle	05-12-89	8
Free Throws Attempted	Dallas @ Los Angeles	05-25-88	12
	Los Angeles @ Detroit	06-12-88	12
Free Throw Percentage	Denver @ Los Angeles	04-23-87	.429

OPPONENTS ALL-TIME INDIVIDUAL RECORDS

Points	Eric Floyd @ Golden State	1987	51
Field Goals Made	Xavier McDaniel @ Seattle	1987	20
Field Goals Attempted	Kareem Abdul-Jabbar @ Milwaukee	1972	37
	Kareem Abdul-Jabbar @ Milwaukee	1972	37
Free Throws Made	Bob Pettit @ St. Louis	1963	15

LAKERS ALL-TIME INDIVIDUAL PLAYOFF RECORDS

FULL GAME

Points	Elgin Baylor	@ Boston	04-14-62	61
Field Goals Made	Elgin Baylor	@ Boston	04-14-62	22
Field Goals Attempted	Elgin Baylor	@ Boston	04-14-62	46
Free Throws Made	Jerry West	vs Detroit	04-03-62	20
	Jerry West	vs Baltimore	04-05-65	20
Free Throws Attempted	Elgin Baylor	vs St. Louis	03-17-60	23
Rebounds	Wilt Chamberlain	@ Chicago	04-19-71	33
Assists	Earvin Johnson	vs Phoenix	05-15-84	24
FT Shooting Pct.	Kareem Abdul-Jabbar	vs Denver	04-25-87	1.000 (12-12)
	Earvin Johnson	@ Phoenix	05-13-90	1.000 (12-12)

ONE HALF

Points	Elgin Baylor	@ Boston	04-14-62	33
Field Goals Made	Elgin Baylor	@ Boston	04-14-62	12
Field Goals Attempted	Elgin Baylor	@ Boston	04-14-62	25
Free Throws Made	Jerry West	vs Baltimore	04-05-65	14
Free Throws Attempted	Earvin Johnson	@ Portland	05-06-85	14
	Jerry West	vs Baltimore	04-05-65	14
	Jerry West	vs Detroit	04-03-62	14
FT Shooting Pct.	Jerry West	vs Baltimore	04-05-65	1.000 (14-14)
Assists	Earvin Johnson	@ Portland	05-03-85	15
Personal Fouls	Jim Krebs	vs Boston	04-21-63	5
	Mitch Kupchak	vs Portland	04-30-85	5
	Mychal Thompson	@ Utah	05-15-88	5
	Michael Cooper	@ Phoenix	05-13-90	5
Rebounds	Wilt Chamberlain	@ Chicago	04-19-71	19

ONE QUARTER

Points	Elgin Baylor	vs Detroit	03-15-61	22
Field Goals Made	Gail Goodrich	vs Golden State	04-25-73	10
Field Goals Attempted	Elgin Baylor	vs Boston	04-1462	13
	Gail Goodrich	vs Golden State	04-25-73	13
	Mike McGee	vs Denver	05-22-85	13
Free Throws Made	Larry Spriggs	vs Dallas	04-28-84	11
Free Throws Attempted	Jerry West	vs Detroit	04-03-62	12
FT Shooting Pct.	Larry Spriggs	vs Dallas	04-28-84	1.000 (11-11)
Assists	Earvin Johnson	vs Denver	05-22-85	10
Personal Fouls	Jim Krebs	vs Boston	04-21-63	5

LAKERS LARGEST VICTORY MARGINS

St. Louis	75	@ Minneapolis	133	03-19-56	58
Los Angeles	126	@ Golden State	70	04-21-73	56
San Antonio	88	@ Los Angeles	135	04-17-86	47
Denver	109	@ Los Angeles	153	05-22-85	44
Dallas	91	@ Los Angeles	134	04-28-84	43
Los Angeles	118	@ San Francisco	78	04-05-69	40
Los Angeles	140	@ Denver	103	04-29-87	37
Phoenix	94	@ Los Angeles	129	04-09-70	35
Boston	104	@ Los Angeles	137	06-03-84	33
Denver	95	@ Los Angeles	128	04-23-87	33
Los Angeles	133	@ Seattle	102	05-25-87	31
Chicago	86	@ Los Angeles	115	04-01-71	29
San Francisco	105	@ Los Angeles	133	04-05-68	28
Phoenix	114	@ Los Angeles	142	04-18-85	28

LAKERS WORST DEFEATS

Los Angeles	114	@ Boston	148	05-27-85	34
Minneapolis	90	@ St. Louis	124	03-21-59	34
Los Angeles	96	@ Boston	129	04-25-65	33
Los Angeles	102	@ Philadelphia	135	06-06-82	32
Los Angeles	110	@ Boston	142	04-18-65	32
Los Angeles	80	@ Utah	128	05-19-88	28
Los Angeles	88	@ Milwaukee	114	04-16-72	26
Los Angeles	101	@ Phoenix	127	04-13-80	26
Los Angeles	86	@ Detroit	111	06-14-88	25
Milwaukee	117	@ Los Angeles	94	04-16-71	23

LAKERS CAREER RECORDS (PLAYOFFS)

Games:	180	by Abdul-Jabbar	Free Throw Pct.:	.831	by Earvin Johnson
Minutes:	6580	by Earvin Johnson	Rebounds:	1783	by Wilt Chamberlain
Points:	4457	by Jerry West	Defensive Reb.:	1088	by Abdul-Jabbar
Scoring Avg	29.1	by Jerry West	Offensive Reb.:	438	by Abdul-Jabbar
Field Goal Att.:	3460	by Jerry West	Assists:	2080	by Earvin Johnson
Field Goal Made:	1643	by Abdul-Jabbar	Blocked Shots:	437	by Abdul Jabbar
Field Goal Pct.:	.592	by Kurt Rambis	Steals:	335	by Earvin Johnson
Free Throws Att.:	1507	by Jerry West	Personal Fouls:	625	by Abdul-Jabbar
Free Throws Made:	1213	by Jerry West	Disqualifications:	24	by Vern Mikkelsen

PLAYOFF RESULTS YEAR-BY-YEAR

	1st Round. Opponent .... W-L	2nd Round Opponent .... W-L	3rd Round Opponent .... W-L	Championship Opponent .... W-L
1961:	Detroit 3-2	St. Louis 3-4		
1962:	Detroit 4-2	....	....	Boston 3-4
1963:	St. Louis 4-3	....	....	Boston 2-4
1964:	St. Louis 2-3			
1965:	Baltimore 4-2	....	....	Boston 1-4
1966:	St. Louis 4-3	....	....	Boston 3-4
1967:	San Fran 0-3			
1968:	Chicago 4-1	San Fran 4-0	....	Boston 2-4
1969:	San Fran 4-2	Atlanta 4-1	....	Boston 3-4
1970:	Phoenix 4-3	Atlanta 4-0	....	New York 3-4
1971:	Chicago 4-3	Milwaukee 1-4		
1972:	Chicago 4-0	Milwaukee 4-2	....	New York 4-1
1973:	Chicago 4-3	G. State 4-1	....	New York 1-4
1974:	Milwaukee 1-4			
1977:	G. State 4-3	Portland 0-4		
1978:	Seattle 1-2			
1979:	Denver 2-1	Seattle 1-4		
1980:	Phoenix 4-1	Seattle 4-1		Philadelphia 4-2
1981:	Houston 1-2			
1982:	Phoenix 4-0	San Antonio 4-0	....	Philadelphia 4-2
1983:	Portland 4-1	San Antonio 4-2	....	Philadelphia 0-4
1984:	K.C 3-0	Dallas 4-1	Phoenix 4-2	Boston 3-4
1985:	Phoenix 3-0	Portland 4-1	Denver 4-1	Boston 4-2
1986:	San Antonio 3-0	Dallas 4-2	Houston 1-4	
1987:	Denver 3-0	G. State 4-1	Seattle 4-0	Boston 4-2
1988:	San Antonio 3-0	Utah 4-3	Dallas 4-3	Detroit 4-3
1989:	Portland 3-0	Seattle 4-0	Phoenix 4-0	Detroit 0-4
1990:	Houston 3-1	Phoenix 1-4		

ALL-TIME LAKERS PLAYOFF SCORING

Player	GP	FGM	FGA	PCT	FTM	FTA	PCT	REB	AST	PF	PTS	AVG
Abernethy	13	22	54	.407	24	29	.828	42	23	18	68	5.2
Abdul-Jabbar	180	1643	3024	.543	784	1037	.756	1525	540	625	4070	22.6
Allen	7	32	82	.390	13	19	.684	32	24	18	77	11.0
Barnes	3	7	19	.386	5	5	1.000	12	2	7	19	6.3
Barnett	28	164	353	.465	135	168	.804	76	71	76	483	16.5
Baylor	134	1388	3151	.440	847	1101	.769	1725	541	445	3623	27.0
Boone	8	37	77	.481	20	21	.952	15	14	28	94	11.8
Boozer	10	65	181	.400	15	20	.750	50	7	20	67	6.7
Branch	11	4	21	.190	6	12	.500	10	5	10	14	1.3
Brewer	1	3	6	.500	0	0	.000	12	4	6	6	0.5
Bridges	17	57	136	.418	38	49	.776	158	29	68	152	8.9
Byrnes	4	1	3	.333	4	6	.667	1	1	0	6	1.5
Campbell	24	37	73	.507	27	38	.711	22	11	42	103	4.3
Carr	10	22	43	.512	5	8	.625	21	40	20	49	4.9
Carter, R.	2	0	1	.000	0	0	.000	0	0	0	0	0.0
Carty	3	0	2	.000	1	3	.333	2	1	3	1	0.3
Chamberlain	80	483	909	.531	299	667	.448	1783	289	226	1265	15.8
Chambers	3	12	33	.522	7	7	1.000	8	1	7	31	10.3
Chaney	11	36	96	.375	16	22	.727	52	48	32	88	8.0
Chones	19	58	135	.430	27	42	.643	121	69	69	1443	7.5
Clark	18	120	268	.448	66	86	.767	60	75	53	306	17.0
Cleamons	6	4	7	.571	0	0	.000	4	4	3	8	1.3
Cooper	168	582	1244	.468	293	355	.825	574	703	474	1581	9.4
Counts	71	203	545	.372	122	160	.763	468	96	227	596	8.4
Crawford	20	38	86	.437	19	36	.528	38	19	45	95	4.8
Dantley	11	70	124	.565	52	69	.754	58	22	33	192	17.5
Egan	34	117	260	.450	73	91	.802	49	92	75	307	9.0
Ellis, B.	16	37	90	.411	22	39	.564	105	18	37	96	6.0
Ellis, L.	56	167	404	.411	108	156	.694	442	42	144	442	7.9
Erickson	60	247	541	.457	74	104	712	267	166	194	568	9.5
Felix	33	92	204	.451	74	102	.725	255	30	125	258	7.8
Finkel	1	0	0	.000	0	0	.000	0	0	0	0	0.0
Ford	20	58	131	.443	28	39	.718	85	44	50	144	7.2

ALL-TIME LAKERS PLAYOFF SCORING CONTINUED

Player	GP	FGM	FGA	PCT	FTM	FTA	PCT	REB	AST	PF	PTS	AVG
Goodrich	73	486	1109	.438	336	412	.816	218	295	198	1308	17.9
Grant	2	4	6	.667	0	0	.000	4	0	1	8	3.0
Gudmundsson	12	16	27	.593	10	15	.667	26	3	23	42	3.5
Hairston	51	220	485	.454	140	177	.791	438	105	126	578	11.3
Hamilton	2	1	3	.333	0	0	.000	2	1	0	2	1.0
Hawkins, C.	5	21	60	.350	12	15	.800	40	16	13	54	10.8
Hawkins, T.	65	194	432	.449	91	155	.587	310	66	198	479	7.4
Hawthorne	3	1	7	.143	4	5	.800	2	2	0	6	2.0
Haywood	11	25	53	.472	13	16	.813	26	4	17	63	5.7
Hazzard	25	95	224	.424	49	72	.681	67	90	69	239	9.6
Hewett	15	61	151	.404	18	29	.621	78	17	40	140	9.3
Holland	10	5	10	.500	4	4	1.000	5	3	8	14	1.6
Hoover	4	2	3	.667	0	0	.000	3	1	3	4	1.0
Horn	7	4	12	.333	4	5	.800	11	2	13	12	1.7
Hudson	9	31	70	.442	11	12	.917	13	17	15	73	8.1
Hundley	53	101	316	.320	68	81	.840	149	157	80	270	5.1
Johnson	14	9	16	.563	2	2	1.000	7	2	9	20	1.4
Joliff	4	6	13	.461	0	0	.000	25	8	4	12	3.0
Jones	7	5	16	.313	2	5	.400	12	0	11	12	1.7
Jordan	5	0	2	.000	0	0	.000	0	6	0	0	0.0
Killum	2	1	1	1.000	2	3	.667	0	0	1	4	2.0
King	28	67	157	.427	31	38	.816	73	61	71	165	5.9
Krebs	11	127	351	.362	75	96	.781	348	53	211	329	5.3
Kupchak	30	44	85	.518	25	42	.595	92	9	60	113	3.8
Kupec	11	8	18	.444	5	7	.714	16	4	7	21	1.9
Lamar	10	12	41	.293	9	10	.900	9	14	12	33	3 3
Lamp	5	3	6	.500	1	2	.500	3	1	3	7	1.4
Landsberger	39	42	113	.372	12	20	.600	150	7	76	96	2.5
LaRusso	n	361	880	.410	312	412	.757	629	162	308	1032	13.4
Lee	8	0	0	.000	2	2	I.000	1	0	2	2	0.7
Leonard	34	130	364	.357	74	98	.755	90	165	77	334	9.8
Lester	9	6	15	400	7	9	..778	3	9	7	19	2.1
Love	2	2	3	.667	2	3	.667	3	1	0	6	3.0
Lucas	14	59	112	.527	14	19	.737	91	10	53	132	9.4
Lynn	8	2	3	.867	0	0	.000	2	1	1	4	1.3
McAdoo	61	340	671	.507	135	189	.714	335	54	195	817	13.4
McCarter	17	30	83	.361	2	7	.286	29	20	32	62	3.6
McGee	50	184	341	.540	57	89	.640	85	38	87	441	8.8
McGill	5	5	9	.556	1	1	1.000	9	2	9	11	2.2
McMillian	44	335	741	.452	139	179	.771	232	81	111	808	18.4
McNamara	8	5	9	.556	1	2	.500	4	0	1	11	1.4
Matthews	22	13	28	.464	14	17	.824	5	11	13	40	1.8
Mix	8	2	5	.400	3	3	1.000	1	0	6	7	0.9
Mueller	14	20	59	.339	5	14	.357	54	18	32	45	3.2
Nater	17	19	38	.500	20	26	.769	40	1	27	58	3.4
Nelson	16	31	66	.470	22	28	.786	72	21	42	84	5.3
Neumann	6	11	29	.379	2	4	.500	2	9	14	24	4.0
Nevitt	7	3	9	.333	4	8	.500	6	1	11	10	1.4
Nixon	58	440	921	.478	142	186	.763	195	464	201	1027	17.7
Price	16	37	107	.346	11	17	.647	31	33	42	85	5.3
Rambis	119	258	436	.592	132	187	.706	627	93	316	648	5.2
Reed	1	2	4	.500	0	2	.000	2	0	2	4	4.0
Riley	34	89	245	.363	23	31	.742	55	45	70	123	3.6
Rivers	6	4	12	.333	7	8	.875	4	6	6	15	2.5
Roberson	13	18	47	.383	10	17	.588	42	4	27	46	2.6
Robinson	7	19	41	.463	7	10	.700	13	6	13	45	6.4
Robisch	8	16	29	.552	6	7	.857	22	3	10	38	4.9
Russell	11	65	157	.414	44	50	.880	48	25	0	174	15.8
Selvy	50	209	524	.399	142	181	.758	222	186	141	560	11.2
Smith	3	42	88	.477	12	17	.706	53	6	20	96	19.2
Smrek	18	3	15	.200	5	9	.556	13	0	19	11	o.s
Spriggs	28	52	102	.510	39	50	.780	67	38	47	143	5.1
Tatum	11	67	134	.500	16	24	.667	54	27	34	150	13.6
Thompson, B.	3	6	11	.545	2	2	I.000	6	2	2	14	4.7
Trapp	10	5	33	242	4	7	.571	16	6	9	20	2.0
Tresvant	11	23	61	.451	19	23	.826	38	16	22	65	6.9
Turner	2	2	5	.400	2	2	I.000	2	0	1	6	3.0
Wagner	5	2	5	.400	2	2	I.000	2	3	3	6	1.2
Warner	5	7	12	583	0	0	.000	9	6	11	14	2.8
Washington	3	5	11	..455	5	7	.714	10	1	0	16	5.0
West	153	1622	3460	.469	1212	1507	.805	855	970	45	4457	29.1
Wiley	27	52	103	.505	16	37	.432	272	34	80	120	4.4
Woolridge	24	79	145	.544	70	99	.707	93	27	70	228	9.5